> "This book is for Maya, the keenest, most daring adventurer we know, who patiently and happily tackles every hike, bike ride, paddling adventure and sailing voyage that our mad 'wild travel story' trio dreams up. She inspires us daily, drives us to do more, and most importantly, makes us laugh.

I0382935

100 THINGS TO SEE IN TROPICAL NORTH QUEENSLAND

By locals Catherine Lawson and David Bristow

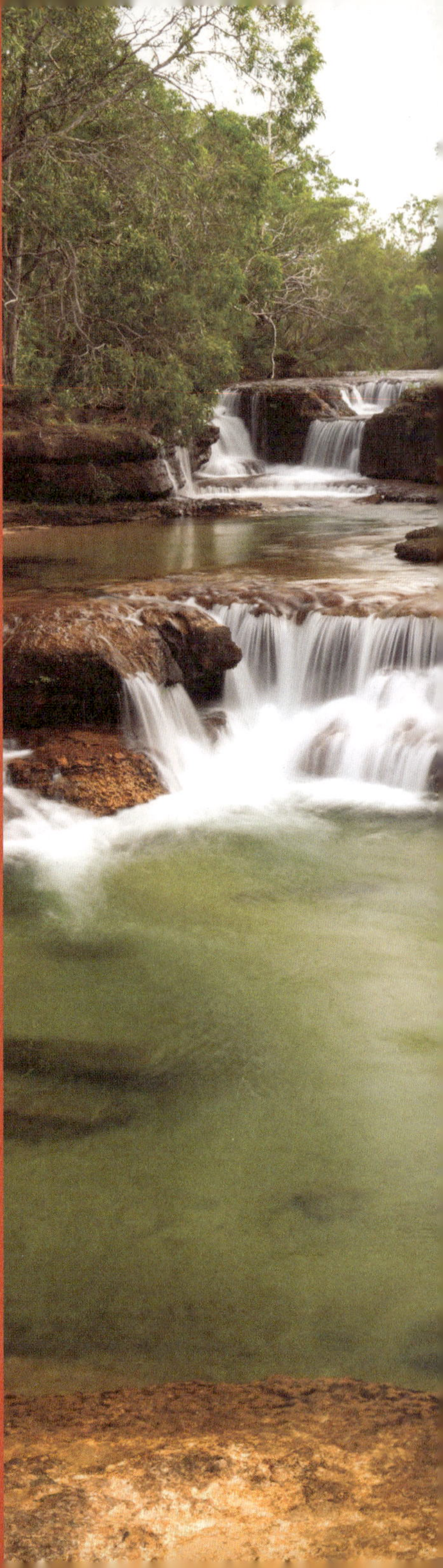

MAPS
Tropical North Queensland

FOREWORD

> As far back as I can remember, while I was a primary school student at Cairns North State School, my mind was always daydreaming about the explorers who first set foot into, what was then, a fairly savage environment. People such as Edmund Kennedy, who in 1848 tried to make it overland from the coast near Dunk Island, all the way up to the top of Cape York Peninsula. Those daydreams actually set me on a course of adventure in the far north, following up not only Kennedy but others such as Ludwig Leichhardt, Christie Palmerston and the Jardines. Needless to say, academic achievement was not high on my list of things to do, and my school reports reflected that situation. Not to worry, it all turned out in the end.
>
> Tropical North Queensland has been my backyard for almost all of my life. Mind you, I did push the boundaries out a bit to include the Top End, the Kimberley and Central Australia, but always, Tropical North Queensland was the springboard for accessing "adventure country".
>
> And the spirit of adventure was not confined to dreaming about the explorers. Back then, in the city of Cairns, there lived an abundance of modern-day adventurers. Cape York had still not been entirely explored, and communities such as Weipa simply did not exist. Crocodile shooters were almost a dime a dozen back then and the Cape and the Gulf of Carpentaria were their hunting grounds. They were all equipped with post World War II .303 rifles which were available for the price of 15 pounds, brand new from the Lithgow Small Arms Factory. I vaguely remember tanned crocodile skins occasionally on display nailed up on the walls of gun-shops in the city. But, by the early 1970s, that era was passed, and these days, the crocodiles do the hunting.
>
> I was lucky enough, later in life, to be based in Townsville with the Australian Army Aviation Corps, and as a result, managed to fly in Kiowa helicopters (jet-ranger helicopters to you civilians) all over northern Australia for 15 years, so I got to know this country of ours very well indeed.
>
> In my mind, Tropical North Queensland is like nowhere else in Australia. Of course, the Kimberley and the Top End are terrific in their own right, and so is the Red Centre. But, none of them has anything like the tropical rainforest environments or a Great Barrier Reef habitat along with coral atolls dotted along the coastline. You only find that up here in TNQ. Likewise, only at The Tip are you lucky enough to also encounter an entirely distinct Indigenous race of people, the Torres Strait Islanders. They have a culture totally different from the mainland Indingous Australians.
>
> Of course, with the Great Barrier Reef and the Torres Strait Islands part of Tropical North Queensland, there is a rich tapestry of history to appreciate, and that's precisely what this publication lends itself too. It's a bit like a field-guide, pointing out all the places of interest and areas to go and explore. Let me assure you, Tropical North Queensland is the part that stands out head and shoulders from the rest.

Les Hiddins, The Bush Tucker Man

Contents

12   Author's introduction

CHAPTER 1
The Great Barrier Reef
16   Snorkel and dive
19   Fly over the GBR
20   Michaelmas Cay
21   Nudey Beach, Fitzroy Island
23   Green Island
24   Frankland Islands
26   Snapper Island
27   Low Isles
28   Undine Cay
29   Lizard Island

CHAPTER 2
Exploring Cairns

34   Cairns Esplanade
35   Trinity Inlet
36   Crystal Cascades
37   Rusty's Markets
38   Hartley's Crocodile Adventures
40   Tropical Thrills
41   Spectacled flying-foxes
42   Cairns Botanic Gardens
43   Skyrail Rainforest Cableway
44   Barron Falls
46   Australian Butterfly Sanctuary
47   Davies Creek Falls
48   Palm Cove
50   Ellis Beach
51   The Gatz, Wangetti Beach

CHAPTER 3
Port Douglas and Daintree

54   Four Mile Beach
56   Dickson Inlet
57   Bally Hooley Rail
58   Port Douglas by sea
60   Port Douglas Markets
61   Wonga Beach
62   Mossman Gorge
65   Daintree River
66   Daintree National Park
70   Marrdja Botanical Walk
72   Cape Tribulation
73   The Bloomfield Track
75   Bloomfield Falls
76   Cedar Bay
78   Home Rule Falls
79   Lions Den Hotel

CHAPTER 4
Cooktown and Cape York

82   Black Mountain
83   Cooktown
84   Endeavour River fishing
85   Grassy Hill Lighthouse
86   Mount Cook
87   Mary Watson's grave
88   Connies Beach, Cape Flattery
90   Quinkan Rock Art
91   Rinyirru (Lakefield) National Park
94   Flinders Island Group
96   Historical Musgrave Roadhouse
97   The Bend, Coen
98   Weipa

CONTENTS

100 Chilli Beach, Iron Range National Park
101 The Old Telegraph Track
104 Kennedy's Lost Camp
105 Captain Billy Landing
106 Twin Falls
108 Mutee Head
109 Seisia
110 The Tip, Frangipani Bay
111 Thursday Island

CHAPTER 5
Cassowary Coast
114 Babinda Boulders
115 Josephine Falls
116 Paronella Park
118 Misty Mountains
119 Mission Beach
120 Djiru National Park
121 Tully Gorge
122 Cardwell Spa
124 Hinchinbrook Island
127 Abergowie State Forest

CHAPTER 6
Atherton Tablelands
130 Hot air ballooning
132 Mareeba Rodeo
133 Granite Gorge
134 Lake Tinaroo
135 Curtain and Cathedral fig trees
136 Mobo Creek Crater
137 Lake Eacham
138 Yungaburra
139 Wongabel Forest and Hasties Swamp

140 Mount Hypipamee
142 The Falls Circuit
146 The Tablelands Food Trail
147 MaMu Tropical Skywalk
148 Big Millstream Falls
149 Wooroonooran National Park

CHAPTER 7
The Wild West
152 Cobbold Gorge
154 Undara Lava Tubes
156 Chillagoe Caves
158 The Savannahlander
160 Mungana Archways
161 Innot Hot Springs
162 O'Briens Creek
164 Karumba
166 Leichhardt Falls
167 Gregory River
168 Lawn Hill Gorge
171 Hells Gate

CHAPTER 7
Travel in the Kimberley
172 Travel advice
182 Maps

192 Acknowledgements

11

AUTHOR'S INTRODUCTION

If I had to name my top 10 reasons for living in Tropical North Queensland's pristine paradise, my love of snorkelling and diving would be number one. I am lucky enough to have on my doorstep what over two million travellers come to experience every year: remote tropical islands and the flourishing coral gardens that crowd the seabed in between.

From white sand beaches, I can dive straight into the turquoise sea to glide over enormous coral bombies just teeming with fish. Any day that I can swim alongside a green sea turtle is a good one, and spotting reef sharks, dugongs, manta rays and moray eels reminds me every day what incredible wonders thrive on the Great Barrier Reef.

But this giant, fragile reef off Tropical North Queensland is much more than a magnificent playground for all our watery adventures. The largest living thing on the planet shapes everything and everyone in Queensland's far north, inspiring our deep connections with nature, teaching our kids about the importance of conservation over the economy, fuelling livelihoods and changing them for the better too. It has instilled in me a deep love of the sea and all that it contains, and a growing passion for protecting it too.

Above the reef, the tropical rainforests that dig their toes into sandy cays and continental isles, or fringe white sand beaches from Cardwell to the tip of Cape York, are equally bewitching. For bushwalkers like me, these dark, crowded forests are mysterious and beautiful, just a little perilous and perfect places to escape to when you crave solitude and solace.

It doesn't matter how far you wander, or how high you climb, it's the rainforests themselves that work their magic, tuning you into tiny, magnificent creatures and flora found nowhere else on earth. The Daintree's ancient Gondwanan forests protect some of the most primitive plants left on the planet, and its deep, azure pools and towering canopies will leave you spellbound.

In 20 years of exploring the great far north, I'm yet to see it all. There remains lofty, distant summits and deep, underwater chasms, faraway pockets of impenetrable forest still untrampled by footprints, and that's just how it should be.

What I have seen – by following Indigenous walking trails, by mountain biking old logging tracks, paddling a sea kayak to deserted slithers of sand, and on sailing adventures

that take me far offshore to seldom-visited reefs – has fostered an infatuation with the tropics that I'll never shake off. If I never need to wear a jumper again, that will be just fine with me!

A lifetime of adventures here has driven my family to inspire other travellers – especially families – into the outdoors and far off the beaten track. With my beloved partner – photographer David Bristow – and our most daring companion, daughter Maya, we established wildtravelstory.com as a free information hub for all travellers, but especially families, who attempt to explore deeper and tackle adventures they never thought possible, and we show them how. It's important to me that as humans, we connect with the natural world, to fall in love with it, because only then will we strive to protect it.

I hope that you fall in love with this patch of paradise too and that the Great Barrier Reef and its rich, rare rainforests change you with every single experience you tackle in Tropical North Queensland. After roaming the world for decades, I still come home to Cairns for all the reasons that you'll discover and, most importantly, for the chance to enjoy a life lived well, outdoors.

Catherine & Dave

Catherine Lawson & David Bristow
wildtravelstory.com

GREAT BARRIER REEF

Cruise across the Coral Sea to find yourself on sheltered white-sand beaches and barely-there cays that rise with the retreating tide to reveal colourful fringes of blooming coral. On the world's largest reef system, unexpected finds are everywhere: tropical rainforests and rugged peaks, skin-tingling waterfalls and granite headlands that slide into deep blue sanctuaries for green sea turtles, dolphins and dugongs too.

From Cairns, a tapestry of coconut-fringed isles, shallow reefs and deep diving drop-offs are within easy reach, so any adventure can be yours. Chopper in for a luxe 5-star stay on Green Island or shoulder a backpack and get castaway on national park islands from Hinchinbrook to faraway Lizard Island, which you can pay for with pocket change. All you need is your snorkelling gear, plenty of reef-friendly sunscreen and a couple of lazy weeks to explore under the sea.

Snorkelling off Fitzroy Island – page 21.

SNORKEL & DIVE THE GBR

A kaleidoscopic patchwork of turquoise and jade, the Coral Sea off Cairns is a hotbed of colourful underwater life.

It's not because it's larger than New Zealand, or that you can see it from Outer Space, what you'll discover once you get wet is what impresses most about Queensland's Great Barrier Reef.

Step off Undine's barely-there sand cay, or Fitzroy Island's idyllic, crushed coral shores to join an endless procession of green sea turtles and harmless reef sharks, cruising over lime and tangerine corals peppered with bright Christmas tree worms and countless, darting tropical fish.

THE GREAT BARRIER REEF
Snorkel and dive

☑ MY GBR TOP 5

☐ 1. Watch the world from the bottom of the ocean. If you're not already certified, you can learn to scuba-dive in just three days.

☐ 2. Spend a night on the reef (midnight at sea is amazing!).

☐ 3. Splurge on 30 minutes of sky time in a helicopter and see a side of the reef you'll never forget.

☐ 4. Swim with dwarf minke whales on Agincourt Ribbon Reefs (liveaboard cruises run from June to July only).

☐ 5. Pitch a tent in paradise: you can camp on Fitzroy, High, Russell or Snapper Islands (off Cairns); Hope, Lizard or faraway Flinders Islands (off Cape York), or Dunk, Goold and Hinchinbrook Islands off Mission Beach.

THE GREAT BARRIER REEF
Snorkel and dive

Reaching the reef is easy. Every morning, high-speed catamarans and leisurely paced sailing vessels visit a string of dive and snorkel sites off Cairns and Port Douglas, some getting you there in under two hours. Reefs at Norman, Saxon, Hastings and Upolu Cay are all well visited, so the further you travel (and the more you pay), the more pristine the coral will be.

Close to Cairns, I love crowd-free Michaelmas Cay for its great flocks of nesting seabirds. At ultra-affordable Fitzroy Island – just 45 minutes by ferry – you can kayak, snorkel, camp and kick out over seagrass beds to encounter hawksbill and green sea turtles grazing in the shallows. If you have the time, overnight liveaboard boats let you linger longer at sea for thrilling night dives and unparalleled quietude.

MAKE IT HAPPEN

Compare reef trips and find your perfect fit at greatbarrierreef.com.au.

THE GREAT BARRIER REEF
Fly over the GBR

FLY OVER THE GBR

Get sky high over the largest living thing on earth.

Helicopters are cool. They dip and dive and swoop us out over the reef, packing thrills and unbeatable views into one gripping adventure. Air time doesn't come cheap, but 30 minutes in the sky is all you'll need to take in dazzling, big-picture scenes of the Great Barrier Reef that simply can't be fathomed from a tour boat.

After decades spent sailing and diving off Cairns, I thought I'd seen the reef at its best. But the colours only visible from great heights simply blew me away: deep cerulean blue that brightens to turquoise in the shallows, paler still where waves wash over luminous, fringing reefs and, studding it all, startling, white sand cays, all utterly deserted.

Most helicopter reef itineraries from Cairns will loop over nearby Arlington Reef and the blissfully unpopulated Upolu Cay, and skim across Vlasoff Reef and its stunning sprinkle of sand, nestled within. Thirty minutes in the sky literally flies by, but helicopter tours are worth every dollar for the unexpected scenes they reveal of the largest living structure on the planet.

HOW BIG?

The Great Barrier Reef is enormous: 2900 reefs, 600 islands and 300 coral cays stretching 2300km along the Queensland coast. The world's biggest reef supports a whopping 10 per cent of all the fish species on earth.

MAKE IT HAPPEN

Book your flight through one of these Cairns-based operators: nautilusaviation.com.au, gbrhelicopters.com.au or helitoursnq.com.au.

THE GREAT BARRIER REEF
Michaelmas Cay

MICHAELMAS CAY
Spend a day on a sand cay that's just for the birds.

I first sailed here searching for a reprieve from howling monsoonal winds. What I found was a haven in every sense: a calm, translucent lagoon fringed by colourful coral reef, and rising above it all, a glistening white sand cay inundated with beautiful, just-out-of-the-nest seabirds.

This solitary sand cay is one of the most important on the reef, providing a sanctuary for local and migratory birds. While much of the cay is off-limits to humans, a viewing area lets you get incredibly close to the birds and their chicks that add a beautiful, albeit noisy, dimension to a day on the reef.

Over summer, up to 20,000 pairs of sooty terns, common noddies, lesser terns and brown boobies call Michaelmas home, and nowhere else on the GBR can you observe them in such numbers. But birds aren't the only thing to enjoy here.

A flourishing mosaic of bombies and plate coral, Michaelmas Reef extends far to the east but starts mere metres from the beach so you can step off the sand and kick out over giant clams, keeping pace with green sea turtles as you explore. Access to the reef is easy, making it an excellent destination for kids and beginner snorkellers to spend a day.

GET YOURSELF THERE

Michaelmas Cay lies 40km northeast of Cairns, about 90 minutes by cruise boat. Ocean Spirit cruises daily to the cay (weather permitting) for snorkelling, scuba diving, and semi-submersible boat rides (oceanspirit.com.au). Boat moorings are available for explorers who arrive by private boat. Island access is only permitted from 9.30am to 3pm. From April to September, southeasterly trade winds protect the cay's northern lagoon.

TRUE STORY

In 1901, a mining operation harvested seabird guano on Michaelmas Cay. In 1975, the tiny isle became its own national park.

THE GREAT BARRIER REEF
Nudey Beach, Fitzroy Island

NUDEY BEACH

Swim with sea turtles and reef sharks off the north's best beach.

Jump aboard a fast ferry out of Cairns, and you can be spreading out your towel at Nudey Beach within the hour. Contrary to its titillating name, Nudey Beach rarely sees a show of flesh. What appeals most about this idyllic slither of crushed coral lies under its waves: great colourful bombies that rise up at low tide, bringing its luminescent parrotfish, wrasse and fusiliers into clear, close view.

There are snoozy blue-spotted rays to find and beautiful batfish hiding beneath shadowy overhangs. Great granite boulders bookend Nudey Beach, and casuarina trees throw shade, making it a top place to hang out for the day if you pick up cold drinks en route.

☑ FITZROY'S TOP 5

☐ 1. Meet the turtles: the island's volunteer-run Cairns Turtle Rehabilitation Centre offers daily hour-long tours (**cairnsturtlerehab.org.au**).

☐ 2. Hike through rainforest to Nudey Beach (600m, 20mins), stopping en route to climb giant granite boulders and peer down at the fringing coral below.

☐ 3. Summit Fitzroy Island's lofty peak for stunning Coral Sea vistas and whale watching over winter (4km, 3hrs return).

☐ 4. Snorkel in solitude off Bird Rock at the far end of Welcome Beach.

☐ 5. Rent a sea kayak and head towards Little Fitzroy Island for superb, all-alone snorkelling.

THE GREAT BARRIER REEF
Nudey Beach, Fitzroy Island

Fitzroy Island is so easy and affordable to reach, but even if it were a million miles away I'd love it just as much for the wilder side it reserves for sea kayakers and hikers who can discover faraway beaches and snorkel snug blue coves, and climb steep rainforested trails for breathless summit vistas.

With an eco-friendly beachfront resort and palm-fringed campground, Fitzroy Island is what five-star Green Island isn't: a laidback destination that everyone can afford, and few can resist. The step-off-the-sand snorkelling and the chance to park your sandy feet at Foxy's beach bar for sunset cocktails, are equally appealing.

There are sailing cruises, SUPs and sea kayaks to rent, and a turtle rehabilitation centre to tour, or you could just slow down. After all, this tropical isle is relaxation central and the cheapest patch of palm-fringed paradise you can get to out of Cairns.

SHHH...

Sneak into the Secret Garden. Follow bright blue butterflies, orange-footed scrub fowls and the coo of imperial pigeons along this interpretive trail to a secret rainforest spot (700m, 30mins return).

GET YOURSELF THERE

Fitzroy Island is located 45 minutes by fast ferry from Cairns. Book a beachfront resort room or campsite at **fitzroyisland.com** (phone 07 4044 6700). The island rents snorkelling gear, SUPs and kayaks, and Foxy's Bar is the place for lunch and sunset drinks. Plan your walks at **parks.des.qld.gov.au**.

THE GREAT BARRIER REEF
Green Island

GREEN ISLAND
Escape for 5-star play or stay for just a day.

By day, this popular slice of paradise is a hive of activity – part theme park, part national park – but come 4pm when the day-trippers depart, sanctuary returns, plunging this 6000-year-old sand cay into glorious solitude. If there's one thing that sets this close-to-Cairns island apart from the rest, it's Green Island's five-star rating.

Luxury is what Green Island does best, so don't miss the chance to indulge in one of the easiest island escapes on the East Coast. Girthed by coral gardens with a surprisingly lush rainforest at its core, Green Island is so compact you can walk around in under an hour. That leaves plenty of time for snorkelling and guided scuba dives, windsurfing lessons and glass-bottom boat tours. And if you want to linger longer, whizz back to Cairns by helicopter.

Curiously for a national park-protected island, Green Island has long been home to the theme park, Marineland Melanesia, where you can ogle Cassius. At 5.48 meters, he's the largest estuarine crocodile in captivity. There are baby crocs to hold, sea turtles to encounter and you can spy on over 100 species of fish, coral and anemones in the aquarium. If it sounds touristy, it is, but don't let that stop you.

MAKE IT HAPPEN

High-speed catamarans from the Cairns Reef Fleet Terminal reach Green Island in around 45 minutes. To stay overnight, book packages at **greenislandresort.com.au**. For day trips, head to **greatadventures.com.au** or **greenisland.com.au**.

FRANKLAND ISLANDS

Discover the place where turtles take sanctuary.

Rainforested and remote, the five coral-fringed isles that form the Frankland Island Group lure travellers south of Cairns with secluded island camping and day trips packed with dives, snorkelling and low-tide discovery tours.

Protected within this island cluster, great green sea turtles take refuge, little disturbed by the day-trippers who arrive at Normanby Island most mornings to kick out over the fringing reef that's renowned for its giant, bright-lipped clams.

Low tide at Normanby brings the coral into closer view, and biologist-led walking tours of the island's fringing rock pools are not to be missed for all the curious creatures you'll spot: small octopus, spider conches, brittle stars and thick, black sea cucumbers.

A world away but right next door, Russell Island will thrill self-sufficient solitude-seekers with Robinson Crusoe-style reef stays at rustic national park campsites.

PITCH A TENT IN PARADISE

Spend a night on Russell Island's lighthouse reserve or take your own boat or sea kayak to my favourite – remote High Island – with one solitary campsite (launch from Mulgrave or Russell River boat ramps). Pack camping gear, food and a stove (no campfires) and book campsites online at parks.des.qld.gov.au.

THE GREAT BARRIER REEF
Frankland Islands

Arrive during the week, and you'll most likely have the entire island all to yourself.

Just one company – Frankland Islands Cruise and Dive – travels daily from Cairns to Deeral Landing (by bus) and on to Normanby Island by ferry for around five hours of water play. You can hire a see-through kayak or SUP, or take a semi-submersible or glass-bottom boat tour. Most visitors spend the day snorkelling, so if you love to dive, do it here for the seclusion you'll experience exploring Normanby's green sea turtle sanctuary and time on the reef that is all your own.

I spotted the largest lionfish of my life while diving off Normanby, nestled in soft corals on the side of a bombie, and lots of amazing turtles viewed with good visibility at a depth of three to six metres.

MAKE IT HAPPEN

Frankland Islands Cruise & Dive travels from Cairns to Normanby Island (10km offshore) daily and transfers campers to Russell Island (**franklandislands.com.au**).

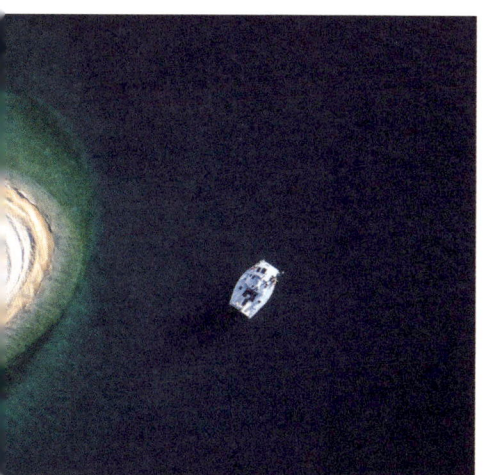

THE GREAT BARRIER REEF
Snapper Island

SNAPPER ISLAND

Paddle to this reef-fringed isle where campers come first.

Forget private-island pampering and expensive exclusivity: paddle to Snapper Island for an adventurous tropical stay without the butlers, buffets and spa treatments. After the 90-minute paddle from Wonga Beach, or 45-minute paddle from Cape Kimberley, you can camp on the sand or string out a hammock on this coral-fringed national park.

Pristine and unpopulated, Snapper Island is fringed by rugged cliffs and a handful of tiny beaches with lush, impenetrable vine forests at its core. For paddlers, this is easily the most accessible isle in the far north and so compact you can explore it in one wonderful day, stopping to snorkel the reef that flourishes off the island's northern fringe.

No trails penetrate the fragile interior, but you can circle the island via beaches and over headlands, and fish the rugged coves off its eastern side.

Four shady beachfront campsites at West Point provide picnic tables, tarp poles and a toilet. Book campsites online and pack camping gear, plenty of drinking water, snorkelling gear and a hammock.

Snapper Island is in the traditional sea country of the Kuku Yalanji. It sits at the mouth of the Daintree River and was named by Captain Cook, because the island resembled a crocodile as he sailed by.

GET YOURSELF THERE

Snapper Island is accessible by sea kayak (allow 45mins to 2hrs) or private boat. Book campsites and plan your trip at **parks.des.qld.gov.au**. Port Douglas Sea Kayak Tours runs small-group day trips. (**portdouglasseakayak.com**)

THE GREAT BARRIER REEF
Low Isles

LOW ISLES

Meet the world's happiest caretaker on this tropical utopia.

Towering above a woolly mop of coconut palms and frangipanis, the lighthouse at Low Isles illuminates a great sweep of coral reef that surfaces at low tide, calming the sea and bridging two tiny islets 13km off the Port Douglas coastline.

By night, its shining light steers ships away, but sailboats return at dawn, lured by the same, ragged reefs where batfish and black-tipped sharks circle for a feed while turtles patiently ignore the snorkellers ogling them through their GoPros.

One of my favourite sailing anchorages, Low Isles is where I can hook up to a mooring and buzz quickly ashore in the dinghy and stroll a truly beautiful beach. Then, when the day-trippers leave, we snorkel 55 acres of reef in complete seclusion (except for that lucky bugger who lives there to keep the light running).

What sets Low Isles apart is evident from afar: it's as pretty as a picture with few crowds and extensive reefs that get more vibrant the further you swim away from the shore. Boats from Port Douglas make full and half-day trips to the isles, and it's easily the best choice for families who can set up on the sand and manage toddlers at the clear blue water's edge.

⦿ SAIL AWAY

Try Sailaway (**sailawayportdouglas.com**) and Wavedancer (**wavedancerlowisles.com**) for full-day trips. Sailaway and Calypso (**calypsoreefcruises.com**) offer half-day trips too.

THE GREAT BARRIER REEF
Undine Cay

UNDINE CAY

Spread your towel on this tiny Cape Tribulation sand cay.

This unpretentious, sprinkling of sand all but disappears with the rising tide, shimmering like an ocean jewel in the opal-blue sea off the Daintree coast. This is one for true underwater explorers because, thankfully, Undine Cay has no pontoon or semi-submersible trips, just unbelievable coral gardens and a lavish diversity of marine life.

Slip beneath the sea, and you'll discover giant clams and an abundance of sea turtles. Swim over forests of gently swaying feather stars where colourful wrasse feed and clownfish hide amongst the protective tendrils of sea anemones.

When I first discovered Undine Cay, I had its coral gardens all to myself. I was so smitten with this isolated patch of wonder that I called it my favourite place on earth. It continues to astound me, and today, Undine is far easier to reach on day trips out of Port Douglas that include a stop at equally impressive Mackay Reef.

WHAT ABOUT MARINE STINGERS?

Tiny, fingertip-sized Irukandji and the much more venomous box jellyfish inhabit Queensland's tropical beaches and reefs from around September until April. They breed up rivers and migrate downstream with wet season downpours to drift along the coast, inflicting extremely painful and sometimes fatal stings if you come into contact with them. Protecting yourself is easy: over the wet season, wear a Lycra stinger suit or wet suit for ocean swims, snorkelling and kayaking. Why? Because box jellyfish – in particular the chironex fleckeri species – can kill you in under five minutes.

SAIL AWAY

Day cruises with Sailaway depart from Port Douglas (sailawayportdouglas.com).

THE GREAT BARRIER REEF
Lizard Island

LIZARD ISLAND

Calling all castaways: are you ready for Australia's most amazing tropical isle?

Shimmering white sand, baby-blue lagoons and coral as far as you can swim: it's difficult to beat far-flung Lizard Island for its outstanding underwater scenes. I once sailed there for a week, and three months later was still under the sea, floating with green sea turtles and spooking reef sharks and moray eels over great gardens of giant, luminescent clams.

Summertime cyclones and coral bleaching events pummeled Lizard Island over four years from 2014 to 2017. Yet, the reefs are recovering, and the diversity of marine life remains outstanding. Most of Lizard's 24 white-sand beaches have step-off-the-sand snorkelling, and the Cod Hole on the famous Ribbon Reefs is close by for divers.

TOP TIP FOR CAMPERS

BYO folding sea kayak to circumnavigate the island, and if your itinerary is loose and you long to sail Cape York, mingle with the Watsons Bay yachties and you might score a berth on a boat sailing north.

Easy to access and full of fish at low tide, the north wall at Watsons Bay is my favourite spot to eyeball harmless reef sharks on the prowl. A secluded bay-hop away, coral bombies crowd the Blue Lagoon, nestled between four extraordinary granite islands with equally idyllic beaches. The best snorkelling lies in the middle of the bay so paddle or motor out, throw an anchor onto a sand patch and leap overboard.

Hike on from the Blue Lagoon and abseil down the rope that drops you onto blissfully remote Coconut Beach where nautilus shells wash ashore. Elsewhere on Lizard, check out Mary Watson's island ruins (read more about Mary Watson on page 87) and climb Cook's Lookout for mind-blowing views and to find the Indigenous ritual site located just below the summit (2 hours return).

Quite unlike any other destination, Lizard Island attracts an incongruous mix of castaways to its national park-protected sanctuary. Five-star resort guests mingle with grotty yachties and fly-in campers who pay in pocket change for their rustic slice of heaven. That's good news for all budgets, and in true Aussie-style, the island's Marlin Bar gathers them all for sunset cocktails and chilly beers on a frangipani-fringed lawn by the sea.

FIVE-STAR SPLURGE

In April 2014, Cyclone Ita all-but levelled five-star Lizard Island Resort, but a $45 million makeover later, luxury has never looked so good. Book rooms and twice-daily flights aboard East Air at lizardisland.com.au.

THE GREAT BARRIER REEF
Lizard Island

🚩 PLAY ROBINSON CRUSOE

Australia's most spectacularly located fly-in campground returns travellers to the simple life with primitive beachfront sites perfectly positioned for snorkelling stints on the famous Clam Garden. Picnic tables, free gas barbecues, a toilet and drinkable bore water are provided by QLD National Parks.

📍 GET ON BOARD

Lizard Island is located 240km north of Cairns. Visit during the May to October dry season when marine stingers disappear, and the snorkelling is sublime.

EXPLORING CAIRNS

If it feels like everyone's on holidays around Cairns, that's because even locals tune into this holiday hub's distinctly laidback vibe.

In Cairns, you'll never watch a sunset on the city waterfront without a tribe of locals sharing the scenery too, and the city is constantly buzzing with all kinds of festivals, music and markets to rev things up for a happy, heady mix of stayers and travellers. The Esplanade Lagoon gathers everyone together to cool things down in the heart of town, and just on the outskirts of the CBD, those long, white sand beaches begin.

You can't beat Cairns for access to rainforest sanctuaries, waterholes and the Great Barrier Reef's coconut-fringed fun. And when you come back in from the wilds, this city soothes weary travellers with seaside watering holes, river-view restaurants and a waterfront just made for watching the sun go down.

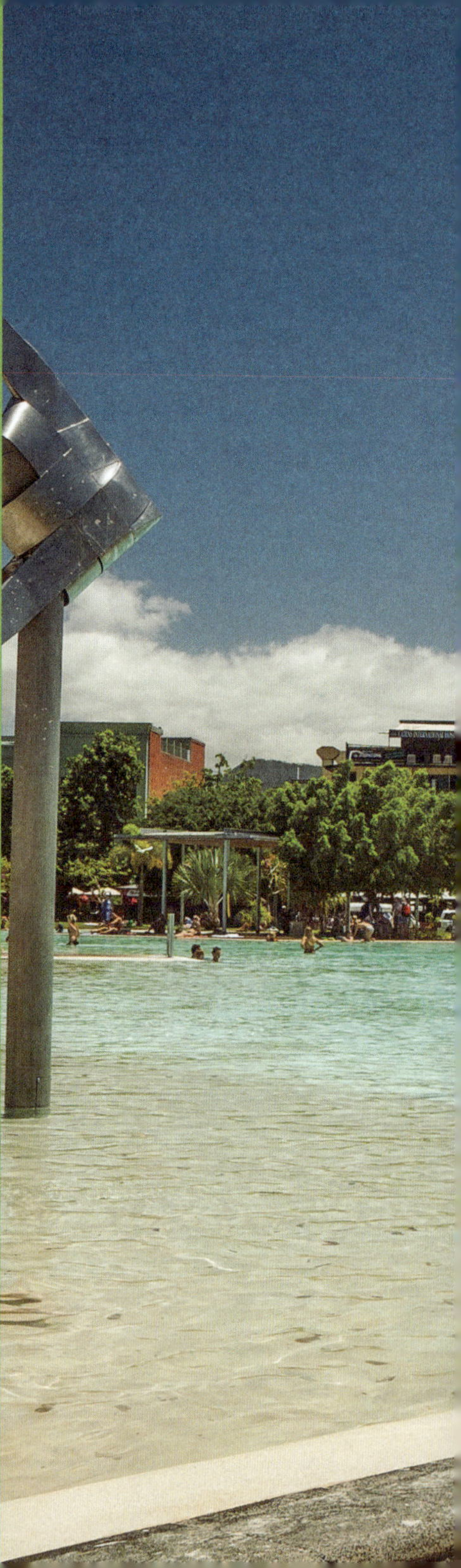

EXPLORING CAIRNS
The Esplanade

THE ESPLANADE
The coolest spot to chill out in Cairns.

It's the hub of outdoor action in Cairns where kids come to play, locals do laps and backpackers lounge on the lawn, staring out over the vibrant tidal mudflats of Trinity Bay. There are playgrounds and markets stalls, music and fitness stations, and because there's no real beach in the city, everybody converges on the saltwater Lagoon to cool down.

Locals and travellers love the Esplanade's free, alfresco fitness classes – everything from aqua Zumba, yoga and Pilates, to skateboarding and rock bouldering sessions. Come the weekend, the Lagoon's shady lawns are transformed with live music and market stalls. There are also free barbecues and plenty of waterfront cafes, bars and restaurants, so you don't have to drift too far from the action.

Not a week goes by that I don't take the plunge, to chill beneath the flying fish fountains that lure everybody to the water's edge. The Lagoon's boardwalk is a top spot to sip coffee and watch the pelicans, mudskippers and crabs as the tide retreats over the mudflats, and the aptly named Muddy's playground is a huge hit with kids.

GET WET

The Lagoon is open from 6am to 9pm (12 noon to 9pm on Wednesdays). Markets are held on Saturdays from 8am to 4pm, and there's live music every Saturday afternoon and all-day Sunday (cairnsesplanade.com.au).

GET MUDDY

For travellers with kids in tow, plan to spend time at Muddy's water and play park, the skate plaza and the rock bouldering zone. All are free and just a short walk north of the Lagoon. You can get a decent coffee at Muddy's Café and some fish and chips for the kids, or make use of the sheltered barbecues tucked around the play equipment (open daily from 9am to 7pm).

EXPLORING CAIRNS
Trinity Inlet

TRINITY INLET
Enjoy a brew with a view, sail, dine, and unwind.

Trinity Inlet's deep, watery wilderness is the place I call home, anchored within easy reach of the city. On any day I might spot dolphins cruising by, crocodiles on the mudflats, sea eagles or stingrays and I'm often on the hunt for barramundi and mud crabs too. To truly experience Cairns, you must spend time riverside. Start by catching a sunset. Do it on the water on a dinner cruise aboard the Spirit of Cairns, or find a breezy seat at the Salt House for the city's coolest harbourside views. You can eat anywhere on the waterfront, but the quirkiest way to sate your appetite is over a bucket of prawns at the Prawn Star – a trio of prawn trawlers that serve up freshly caught seafood and chilled beers at Marlin Marina.

For the best local brews, head upstream to Hemingway's Brewery to sample a genuinely tropical schooner of your choice or try them all on a beer tasting tour (Saturdays and Sundays at 3pm). Right next door, the excellent Fig Tree Playground is where kids go wild, so pack a picnic or fire up the free barbecues.

If you've got barramundi on your mind, you can hire a self-drive fishing pontoon boat from the marina (no licence required). Or join one of a handful of small private charters that fish my favourite spots deep in the mangroves up Trinity Inlet.

FEELING ADVENTUROUS?

Cairns Yacht Club welcomes newbie sailors on its Trinity Inlet sunset sails every Wednesday afternoon. Register online and be at the CYC Boatshed at the Marlin Marina at 12 noon to pay your day membership and join a crew (**cairnsyachtclub.com**).

EXPLORING CAIRNS
Crystal Cascades

CRYSTAL CASCADES

Snorkel with jungle perch in the waterhole Cairns' locals love most.

Close to Cairns and spine-tingly cool, this magnificent little waterway is my go-to spot when I need a rainforest fix and a refreshing dip. The tumbling cascades and deep swimming holes are maddeningly translucent, and if you follow the Ulysses butterflies that flit upstream, you'll find your way to increasingly secluded rock pools.

Dropping swiftly, Upper Freshwater Creek slides through a steep, narrow valley that's overhung with giant fig trees and draped with intricate vines shading this deeply relaxing scene. Where the water stills in swirling pools, jungle perch gather to nibble toes and tease the snorkellers stalking them underwater.

You can climb and rock-hop upstream to shred your swimmers on smooth granite slides, or find a rope swing and get some air. Most who come are content to float about on pool toys, staring up into the rainforest canopy and lazing the day away. But if you need some adventure, hike the short trail to Fairy Falls for an unbeatable Insta-worthy shot.

Popular with locals on weekends, Crystal Cascades is deserted in the early hours and is utterly invigorating over the wet season, especially when it rains just a little.

GET WET

Crystal Cascades is located at Redlynch, 17km from the Cairns CBD. Drive or bike and pack a picnic (toilets, gas barbecues and picnic shelters provided). En route to the falls, kids can burn off extra energy at Goomboora Playground, an adventure playground with a flying fox, bike paths and rope swings over clear swimming holes, downstream of Crystal Cascades. You'll find it signposted off the Western Arterial Road (turn left at Cool Waters Holiday Park).

FIND FAIRY FALLS

Follow the forest trail that shoots off from the left-hand side of the car park. Stick to the creek and climb until you reach the falls (10-15 minutes, one way).

EXPLORING CAIRNS
Rusty's Markets

RUSTY'S MARKETS
Sip a green coconut and snap up exotic tropical fruit.

It's where the locals go when they run out of rambutans or ripe Bowen mangoes, and the quality produce and prices are the best in the country. Big call I know, but Rusty's is one of the things that makes Cairns so liveable, and for fresh food in the north, you won't find a better place to shop.

There are organic fruits and tropical herbs, sourdough bread and locally caught seafood, fresh flowers and nuts and delicious vegan pastries. But far more than a market place, Rusty's is where people in Cairns meet up with their mates. It could be for coffee at dawn (before an early-morning shop), or over a lunchtime laksa or Saturday afternoon smoothie. It's all washed down with cool tunes while dining al fresco in a sea of smiling faces high on the heady aromas of good food.

If you like freshly cooked Asian cuisine, you'll love Rusty's, and you can try before you buy, nibbling samples of exotic tropical fruits as you tick off your shopping list.

WHERE & WHEN?

Stalls at Rusty's Markets fill the entire block from Sheridan Street to Grafton Street in the CBD. Open from Friday to Sunday, from 5am to 6pm. Bargain hunters will score big discounts by shopping just before closing time at 3pm Sunday (**rustysmarkets.com.au**).

HARTLEY'S CROCODILE ADVENTURES
Eyeball the hunter at the top of the food chain.

Smart, powerful, spectacular survivors, estuarine crocodiles are easily the most impressive creatures in the north. Getting close to crocs is an amazing thrill, so when friends and family come to Cairns, I take them to Hartley's Crocodile Adventures.

EXPLORING CAIRNS
Hartley's Crocodile Adventures

TRUE STORY

From the 1940s to the 1960s, crocodiles in Australia were hunted to the brink of extinction for their skins and for sport. In 1974, all Aussie crocs became protected by law.

If you are yet to encounter a feeding estuarine crocodile up-close, a boat cruise on Hartley's Lagoon will get you far, far closer to a croc than you'd usually want to be. Motoring across the lagoon, you won't notice the salties hovering just below the surface until they suddenly sidle alongside your tiny boat and propel themselves skyward, snapping their formidable jaws around the breakfast that's dangling from your guide's outstretched bamboo pole.

You'll jump, someone will yelp, and Australia's largest, most proficient predator will do what it does best: impress everyone on board with incredible displays of speed, agility and strength. Adrenaline-rushes aside, Hartley's showcases all kinds of tropical creatures, including southern cassowaries that you can hand feed.

Beyond the boating lagoon are 10 hectares of wetlands and woodlands to wander through, spending time with koalas, wallabies, quolls and all kinds of fascinating snakes, spiders and scorpions. You'll need a half-day to meet as many animals as you can, and catch at least one crocodile feeding show.

SPEND THE DAY

Hartley's Crocodile Adventures is located at Wangatti, 40km north of Cairns on the Captain Cook Highway, open 8.30am to 5pm daily. Arrive early to beat the heat and get onto the first boat cruise of the day when crocs are hungry (**crocodileadventures.com**).

39

EXPLORING CAIRNS
Tropical thrills

TROPICAL THRILLS
Spike your adrenalin and do something that scares you.

My favourite far northern thrills are the ones that I can tackle myself (without a guide and a credit card). And despite this coastline's somewhat croccy reputation, sea kayaking adventures top my list.

With 2-3 weeks up your sleeve, you can island-hop from Cardwell to Cairns, making camp at Hinchinbrook, Goold and Dunk Islands, Mission Beach, then the Frankland and Fitzroy Islands before pulling into Cairns (time your trip for the dry season months). If time is short, it takes just a day to paddle the usually calm bay off Palm Cove to nearby Double Island. Or in less than an hour, you can push off from Cape Kimberley and reach Snapper Island on the edge of Daintree National Park.

If lofty day hikes are more your thing, the spectacular Devils Thumb (known as Manjal Jimalji) is a top peak to bag, studding the range above Whyanbeel, north of Mossman (10.6km, 8hrs return). Mountain biking the historic Bump Track rounds off my top three and rates as one of Australia's top 10 rides, plunging 6km off the Macalister Range north of Kuranda into the Mowbray River valley.

EXPLORING CAIRNS
Spectacled flying-foxes

SPECTACLED FLYING-FOXES
Meet the sky puppies.

Rainforest trees have evolved to lure spectacled flying-foxes in, pumping out floral scents in the cool of night and growing white flowers that are easily visible to the nocturnal bats after dark.

They sip the nectar and feast on fruit, dropping seeds and spreading pollen that sustains these lofty rainforest trees. It's as much a keystone species as the cassowary, but a little less loved.

In Cairns, their favourite roost sits on prime real estate in a sea of big chain hotels. An entire city may have grown up around them, but the flying-foxes have lingered, clinging to a diminishing canopy of giant strangler figs.

In 2018, a mass culling of trees on private land adjacent to the Cairns City Library forced the bats into an overcrowded canopy of remaining trees. When a heatwave hit Cairns in late 2018, 23,000 spectacled flying-foxes died – around 30 per cent of Australia's population. Only then were they declared endangered.

Some fear the protection may have come too late, but the city's long-standing colony is clinging on, and their roost is a popular tourist attraction. Do visit: the more people who enjoy our much-maligned mega bats, the better.

🗨 JOIN A BAT CHAT

During local school holidays, free, volunteer-led Bat Chats are held on Saturday evenings at 5.30pm at the Cairns City Library on Abbott Street. Find more on facebook **@BATSOCinc.** Find out more about spectacled flying-foxes at **cafnec.org.au**.

EXPLORING CAIRNS
Cairns Botanic Gardens

CAIRNS BOTANIC GARDENS

Hike, bike and spot butterflies and bush tucker in the city's best green space.

With flamboyant tropical gardens and bird-fringed lagoons, this enormous green zone is where travellers and locals mingle, exploring, exercising and relaxing beneath a steamy jungle canopy. Birders wander the wetlands, people-watchers stir their coffees, and kids go wild in the imaginative Nature Playground, building palm-frond huts and looking for fairies hidden in tree trunks.

There are pioneer-era bamboo forests and a butterfly-filled conservatory to explore, full of blooming purple orchids and pitcher plants slowly digesting their prey. I love the gardens for early morning trail runs that begin in the gardens and climb Lumley Hill into Mount Whitfield Conservation Park for Coral Sea views that stretch all the way to Green Island.

Offering much more than a cool escape from the heat, this enormous oxygen-maker provides a great backdrop for all kinds of free community events too: art exhibitions, guided talks and walks, music festivals and more.

BREATHE THE AIR

Head north along Sheridan Street and take the signposted turn onto Collins Ave, just before the airport. Find out what's happening in the gardens at **cairns.qld.gov.au**.

MY TOP TRAIL

Run or walk the Red Arrow Circuit at first light, spooking red-legged pademelons en route to the top (1.5km return).

EXPLORING CAIRNS
Skyrail Rainforest Cableway

SKYRAIL RAINFOREST CABLEWAY

Take this thrilling treetop adventure to the edge of Barron Gorge.

Dangling you high above the rainforest as you glide up the McAllister Range to Kuranda, Skyrail's intimate gondola rides offer big-sky views and access to secluded walking trails and lookouts that will blow you away. The thrilling rush of peering down into the forest makes this much more than a great way to get to Kuranda. The gondolas stop at two hilltop stations en route for rainforested walks to lookouts poised 265 metres above rugged Barron Gorge.

When you finally reach Kuranda, the overwhelming aroma of good coffee and food will greet you, so fuel up and get set to shop or tour one of Kuranda's excellent wildlife parks. I love the Australian Butterfly Sanctuary, but there are more places than you could see in a day: Birdworld, Koala Gardens or Rainforestation Nature Park.

If you love to shop, the locally-grown coffee beans and rainforest honeys are popular take-home choices. Given Kuranda's origins as an artistic hub, the Indigenous painted canvases and wearable art can be irresistible too. The final thrill for the day is getting back to Cairns. Jump back on the Skyrail or return via a different route aboard Kuranda Scenic Railway which journeys across historical 125-year-old bridges and through 15 hand-made tunnels en route to Cairns.

TRUE STORY

Occupied by Indigenous Djabugay people for more than 10,000 years, Kuranda is known as Ngunbay, meaning the place of the platypus. You might spot a platypus in Kuranda, but if you don't, Petersons Creek in the heart of Yungaburra is the most reliable place in the north to see them in the wild.

MAKE IT HAPPEN

Get on the Skyrail Rainforest Cableway at Smithfield, a 20-minute drive north of Cairns City (open 8.45am to 5.15pm, **skyrail.com.au**). Kuranda Scenic Railway heads out of Cairns at 8.30am and 9.30am daily, departing Kuranda for the return journey at 2pm or 3.30pm (**ksr.com.au**).

EXPLORING CAIRNS
Barron Falls

BARRON FALLS
Stand before the far north's most impressive waterfall.

From the high slopes of Mount Hypipamee, the Barron River winds 60km across the Atherton Tablelands, gathering strength before plunging 265m over the edge of Barron Gorge. Spectacular after wet season downpours, Barron Falls' gentler, wintertime flow captivates too. My favourite way to see it is from the vertigo-inducing lookout that overhangs the gorge at the end of the Budaadji Canopy Walk.

This 600m-long, elevated boardwalk lifts you high into the treetops to eyeball epiphytes and fat, curling vines before the thunderous sound of the falls lures you to the edge of Barron's airy abyss. If this easy trail leaves you wanting more, take your walking shoes to Speewah Campground to explore ancient Indigenous pathways and historical pioneering tracks.

◉ UP AND AWAY

Getting to Barron Gorge is half the fun: drive the steep, winding Kuranda Road or jump aboard the Kuranda Scenic Railway or the thrilling Skyrail.

◉ CLIMB INTO THE CANOPY

Kuranda is located 20km northwest of Cairns (turn off the Captain Cook Highway at Smithfield and head up the range). From Kuranda, drive 3.5km along Barron Falls Road and follow the signs to the Barron Falls car park. If you are camping, Speewah Campground is perfect for compact rigs (10km from Kuranda off the Kennedy Highway).

EXPLORING CAIRNS
Australian Butterfly Sanctuary

AUSTRALIAN BUTTERFLY SANCTUARY

Wander amongst fluttering butterflies in Australia's largest aviary.

To sparkle and shine against the dark, lush green of a tropical rainforest, butterflies must be big, bold and beautiful, and none do it better than the multicoloured Cairns birdwing. Its 16cm-wide wings make it Australia's largest. Rivalling the birdwing with its electric blue beauty, the brilliant Ulysses butterfly is equally captivating. So, if you thought it was difficult to get excited about bugs, prepared to get carried away inside this unique Kuranda sanctuary.

In Australia's largest aviary there are butterflies aplenty, 1500 or more all feeding and breeding and colouring the air in dramatic flashes of emerald green and sunny yellow, and landing on hats and shoulders to the delight of visitors. There are intriguing free tours and quiet corners to sit and butterfly-gaze, but what really sets this sanctuary apart is what it releases into the wild: captive-bred butterflies to bolster local populations after damaging cyclones and dry spells.

TOP TIP

Wear a white, red or hot pink shirt to lure the butterflies to land on you.

TRUE STORY

From Townsville to Cooktown, forests of the Wet Tropics World Heritage Area nurture more than 60 per cent of Australia's butterfly species. Two top places to spot them are at Babinda Boulders (60km south of Cairns) and Cape Tribulation in Daintree National Park.

MAKE THE TRIP

The Australian Butterfly Sanctuary is located in Kuranda, close to the Skyrail terminal. It's open daily from 9.45am to 4pm (**australianbutterflies.com**).

EXPLORING CAIRNS
Davies Creek Falls

DAVIES CREEK FALLS

Head for the hills to this granite spa pool, high above Cairns.

Forming a formidable backdrop west of the city, the rugged Lamb Range rises steeply to meet the Tablelands, topped by the rock pinnacles and eucalypt-covered ridges of distant Dinden National Park. Few crowds gather this far off the Kennedy Highway, so the stunning spa pools that fill beneath Davies Creek Falls can be all yours.

Davies Creek Falls is a spectacular sight, plunging 75m over a towering granite rock face and cascading through clear, sandy swimming holes just perfect for summertime chilling. The national park is well within reach for day trips, but it's a difficult destination to leave. If you decide to stay, camp on the edge of Davies Creek, or head further upstream into Dinden National Park to superior waterfront camps shaded by a towering canopy of eucalypts.

Close by, my favourite hiking trail cuts a steep path to Kahlpahlim Rock. It climbs rainforested gullies and rocky knolls blooming with alpine plants to reach the highest point on the Lamb Range and a stunning summit vista over Cairns (12.2km/5 hours, carry plenty of water).

⦿ STAY AND EXPLORE

To reach Davies Creek from Cairns, climb the range to Kuranda, drive 21km west and take the signposted turn-off to Davies Creek and Dinden National Parks. The final 14km of dirt is suitable for 4WD vehicles only. Book campsites in advance with QLD National Parks.

EXPLORING CAIRNS
Palm Cove

PALM COVE
For the best slice of beach life, put yourself in one of the prettiest scenes in the tropics.

Nestled against an imposing backdrop of lush, rainforested hills, a golden sweep of sand arcs around Palm Cove which is fringed by shaggy-topped coconut palms and enormous melaleuca paperbark trees. These throw shade over a relaxed beachfront of boutique hotels, sassy bars and elegant restaurants that make Palm Cove famous, but it's the cove itself - studded with dreamy offshore isles - that completes the canvas.

Palm Cove's five-star stays lure a well-heeled crowd, and the kids playing beachside and the local anglers jigging for squid off the old town jetty keep everything real. A caravan park at the northern end of the esplanade reserves a rich slice of beachfront exclusively for campers. This incongruous crowd stops Palm Cove from sliding into pretentiousness and creates the easy beach holiday vibe that locals love.

Only at Palm Cove could you weave sea kayaking and spa treatments into one indulgent day. And while there are plenty of luxurious spots to sip a sundowner by the beach, when we gather for sunset drinks, it's always on the big front deck at the Surf Club.

🔺 TOP TRIP

Hire a sea kayak on Palm Cove's Esplanade and paddle 30 minutes across to Double Island (teens will love it). Need a guide? Join a paddling and snorkelling tour that loops across the cove to Scout's Hat too.

📍 BEACH YOURSELF

Palm Cove is located 20km north of Cairns and has easy access to the reef and tourist attractions around Kuranda. Accommodation ranges from five-stars (try The Reef House, Alamanda or Peppers) to no stars (camp at NRMA Palm Cove Holiday Park).

EXPLORING CAIRNS
Ellis Beach

ELLIS BEACH
Escape to this tropical haven for sun, sand and surf.

Ellis gets my nod as the most picturesque beach around Cairns, loved by locals for its calm, clear cove and as a top place for weekend picnics beneath the mango trees. It's where I go to bodysurf the breakers and sip coffee with my feet dug into the sand, and when the weather warms up, gather sticky sweet mangoes from the trees that shade the beach.

Ellis is also where you grab your road trip coffees before tackling the north's most scenic coastal drive, from Palm Cove past nudist-friendly Buchans Beach and on to Port Douglas. The café-bar that fronts the beach caters to an eclectic crowd of tourists, tradies and weekend bikers, and serves killer breakfasts with live music all weekend long. The gentle swell off Ellis Beach is kid-friendly and usually calm, and the region's only absolute beachfront caravan park provides cabins and ultra shady campsites with unbeatable ocean views.

GET YOURSELF THERE

Follow the Captain Cook Highway past Palm Cove to Ellis Beach and if you stay, book a cabin or campsite at **ellisbeach.com**.

EXPLORING CAIRNS
The Gatz, Wangetti Beach

THE GATZ
See how your stone creations stack up on Wangetti Beach.

North of Palm Cove where the Captain Cook Highway winds its way to Port Douglas, steep cliffs rise inland, and palm-fringed curls of sand and pebbles give way to the Coral Sea. The seascapes on this scenic coastal drive tug for your attention but none so much as the balancing rock cairns known as The Gatz on Wangetti Beach.

This Insta-worthy art canvas literally stops traffic, luring travellers off the road to gather sea-smoothed stones and build towering and tiny balancing rock creations stacked spectacularly against the sea. It's collective and ever-changing, and while cyclones and gravity do their best to tumble the rock cairns, there's always a fresh artist to build them back up again in some new, imaginative way.

The Gatz is located at the southern end of Wangetti Beach, home to Hartley's Crocodile Adventures and Rex Lookout where hang-gliders launch themselves out over the sea. To the north, there are phenomenal stretches of sand at Oak and Thala Beaches where you might spot dolphins and turtles just offshore. Keep an eye out for crocs amongst the mangroves as you cross the Mowbray River (a popular fishing spot) before ending the road trip at Port Douglas.

⚠ SEASCAPE SCULPTURES

You can't miss the rock cairns at the southern end of Wangetti Beach where there's just enough room to pull off the highway.

PORT DOUGLAS AND THE DAINTREE

Port Douglas is a microcosm of tropical style and regardless of how laidback it gets, the locals and visitors never fail to keep things classy.

Port is a top little place to spend up big. The reef is oh-so-close, and deserted tropical cays are just an hour's sail away. The fishing off Port is nothing short of incredible and the boats that cruise and charter out of here are renowned for their personalised, small-group experiences.

When you drive north into the Daintree, the rainforest stays, walks and waterholes will waylay you once again. The Daintree's ancient tropical canopies will dazzle you, and the hope of glimpsing a southern cassowary will lure you along boardwalk trails to the edge of crystal streams and deep, blue pools.

Rex Smeal Park, at the mounth of Dixon Inlet – page 56.

FOUR MILE BEACH
Ride a bike on this famously firm stretch of golden sand.

There's nothing else like it in the north: a beach so long it runs the entire length of town, squeezed between a ragged fringe of casuarinas and bush almond trees, and the deep blue beyond. Famously firm, Four Mile Beach is flat and fit to ride a bike on, providing one of the most beautiful cycleways you are ever likely to enjoy.

The shallow seabed offshore creates perfectly calm conditions for stand-up paddleboarding and swimming, and this big, broad beach that curls away south provides a beautiful backdrop for early morning walks to the Sky Deck that hangs out over the Coral Sea atop Flagstaff Hill.

Four Mile Beach is where the best relaxing takes place in Port Douglas, but when people head back into town to park their sandy feet under café tables and bars, they take the beach's seriously

PORT DOUGLAS & DAINTREE
Four Mile Beach

🛈 FAVE HIKE

Hit the beach at first light, climb the stairs up Flagstaff Hill to the Sky Deck for sublime sunrise views, and loop across the headland to Dickson Inlet where you can salute the sun and build your own balancing rock cairn.

laidback undertow with them. Studded with coconut palms and oh-so-close to the reef, Port (as the locals call it), is one of the most idyllic holiday destinations in the state. It seduces travellers with a tropical cocktail of lazy beach time, sunset seafood dinners and soothing island escapes.

Despite its five-star reputation, this tiny headland sandwiched between Dickson Inlet and Four Mile Beach offers lots of down-to-earth adventures, and it's my favourite place to spot crocs, sip a beer and shop.

📍 GET YOURSELF THERE

Follow the Captain Cook Highway 68km north of Cairns. Plan your stay at **visitportdouglasdaintree.com**.

PORT DOUGLAS & DAINTREE
Dickson Inlet

DICKSON INLET

Spot wildlife on this croccy, calm water cruise.

With Port Douglas as your base, this mangrove-fringed inlet is all the wild you'll need to spot crocs and shipwrecks and sip something sparkling as you glide upriver in search of sunbirds and sea eagles.

Two local boats – the old Lady Douglas paddle steamer and the Choo Choo Explorer – take small group adventures up Dickson Inlet and Packers Creek. Their 90-minute cruises are not only great value but perfect for days when the sea whips up offshore.

Both provide an excellent chance of spotting the estuarine crocodiles that hide amongst the mangroves and haul out on muddy banks to warm themselves over the wintery May-to-November dry season. There's plenty of history to unearth along the way, and kids love to cruise aboard the Lady Douglas for the chance to take the wheel and give parents a scare.

⚑ CLIMB ABOARD

Boat tours depart Crystalbrook Superyacht Marina, daily over the peak winter travel season. Choose the Lady Douglas (**ladydouglas.com.au**) or combine a trip on the Bally Hooley with a Choo Choo Explorer cruise (**ballyhooleyrail.com.au/choo-choo-explorer**).

PORT DOUGLAS & DAINTREE
Bally Hooley Rail

BALLY HOOLEY RAIL
Ride the train that's all puff.

Every Sunday the Bally Hooley Railway is full steam ahead, mustering trainspotters and youngsters with its piercing whistle for an historical jaunt along 100-year-old tracks. This cheap thrill runs between Crystalbrook Marina and St Crispins Station, and a return trip takes just an hour. To extend the exploring, team your ride with a wildlife-spotting cruise on Dickson Inlet that sets off from St Crispins Station.

TAKE A RIDE

The Bally Hooley's old steam engine operates only on Sundays, but diesel-fuelled rides are available from Wednesday to Saturday over the peak winter travel season (9.30am-3pm, **ballyhooleyrail.com.au**).

57

PORT DOUGLAS BY SEA

Explore offshore for watery fun on and under the sea.

Floating in the sea off Four Mile Beach may be some kind of bliss, but sooner or later that distant horizon will beckon, and when it does, head for the other side of town where cruise boats await to whisk you away to opalescent reefs and barely-there sand cays.

An hour's sail away, Low Isles is the easiest snorkelling site to reach (and an uber-pretty one at that), but don't stop your discoveries there. You can ogle fish off Undine Cay, Mackay Reef, Opal Reef or visit Quicksilver's Agincourt Reef pontoon all in a day, or tackle wilder, multi-day undersea adventures on a liveaboard cruise to the faraway Cod Hole and the Ribbon Reefs near Lizard Island.

If time or money is short, a sunset sail is an unbeatable choice. With a cool breeze on your face, the setting sun at your back and the deep, blue yonder firmly in your sights, sailing during the north's golden hour is some kind of magic. A handful of

PORT DOUGLAS & DAINTREE
Port Douglas by Sea

companies offer end-of-day cruises (with bubbles and beer), but if you've already blown your budget, this top little travel hack will get you out on the water without spending a cent.

Every Wednesday afternoon, local Port Douglas sailors invite complete strangers aboard their boats for sunset sails that loop out of Dickson Inlet into the Coral Sea. You don't need to be experienced, just over 18 years old, and get yourself to the Port Douglas Yacht Club by 4pm to sign in and find yourself a skipper.

Yachts set sail around 4.30pm for a couple of hours of sunset fun before heading back to the club for drinks and dinner. It's free and fun and the best way I know to get out on the water without opening your wallet.

SET SAIL

Port Douglas is located 68km north of Cairns (about an hour's drive). To choose your best reef and island getaway, check out the reef guide at **visitportdouglasdaintree.com**. For free WAGS (Wednesday Afternoon Go Sailing) fun, head to the Port Douglas Yacht Club on Dickson Inlet at 4pm on any Wednesday (**portdouglasyachtclub.com.au**).

PORT DOUGLAS & DAINTREE
Port Douglas Markets

GET SHOPPING

The Port Douglas Markets is held every Sunday at Rex Smeal Park (at the mouth of Dickson Inlet, page 56) from 8am to 1.30pm (**douglas.qld.gov.au**).

PORT DOUGLAS MARKETS

Shop alfresco for tropical treasures to wear, hang, eat and enjoy.

Lured by the heady aroma of frangipani and good coffee into a vibrant maze of pop-up stalls, blissed-out travellers gather on the ocean's edge for alfresco shopping with a distinctly tropical taste. The Sunday morning crowd swells around 10am, but there's no hustle and bustle in this sea of tranquil shoppers who sip coconuts and stop for massages, to rejuvenate wardrobes with more colourful creations and fill their shopping bags with fresh, locally-grown tropical fruits.

Fossick amongst the stalls selling croc-teeth jewellery and hand-painted silk sarongs to discover the photographers and artists whose work captures the north's most remarkable natural scenes.

Port Douglas is famous for being the kind of place where you can eat with sand on your feet. When your bags are full, and you've had your fill of mango ice cream and chocolate-covered bananas, rest your feet at one of my favourite watering holes.

On market day, I love to join the Sunday scene at the Court House Hotel for live tunes and ales and a menu diverse enough to please healthy vegetarians like me. Afterwards, as the sun dips low, grab a waterfront table at The Tin Shed for the best sunset views in town to watch the day disappear over the range.

PORT DOUGLAS & DAINTREE
Wonga Beach

WONGA BEACH
Slow your pace at this local secret spot.

With famously good fishing on the edge of the Daintree River, this quiet, coconut-fringed beach is a dream destination for beachcombers and boaties. There are easy-to-access, protected reefs just offshore and 140km of river to explore on the edge of Daintree National Park.

Launch your boat from Wonga Beach Caravan Park or south at Dayman Point to explore nearby Snapper Island (see page 26).

Accommodation at Wonga Beach is so far limited to a handful of B'n'Bs, holiday rentals and caravan parks, which means uncrowded fun as you fish off Cape Kimberley or up the Daintree River where big barramundi, mangrove jack, fingermark, queenfish and grunter await.

TOP TIP

When I lived at Wonga Beach, every day began with a bike ride and beach walk, and just-out-of-bed beachcombers are likely to spot manta rays and green sea turtles cruising the calm, blue bay.

BEACH YOURSELF

Wonga Beach is located 90km north of Cairns (30km north of Port Douglas). When you visit, don't miss a waterhole swim at nearby Mossman Gorge.

PORT DOUGLAS & DAINTREE
Mossman Gorge

MOSSMAN GORGE

Chill your bones in the Daintree's most beautiful chasm.

From the rugged, uninhabited slopes of the Mount Carbine and Mount Windsor Tablelands, Mossman River beats a hasty retreat to the sea. It plunges through the rainforest, carving out its sheer granite gorge and tossing aside great granite boulders.

In the dry season when the river loses vigour, travellers arrive to wind down and cool off, lounging in Mossman's clear, deep pools where schools of hungry jungle perch tease snorkellers and nibble toes. Without these idyllic, ice-cold swimming holes, this pristine corner of traditional Kuku Yalanji land in Daintree National Park may never have entered the spotlight.

SUP THE RAINFOREST

Ride a stand-up paddleboard up the Mossman River on a half-day guided adventure (visit windswell.com.au).

PORT DOUGLAS & DAINTREE
Mossman Gorge

But the word is out and Mossman Gorge's bushwalking trails and heavenly, secluded pools are firmly on the map. The best way to experience the gorge is to arrive early – before 10am – or after 3pm. Rainy days deter the masses too, as does exploring deeper into the park on foot, chasing ubiquitous Ulysses butterflies far upstream to pools where platypus and freshwater turtles hide.

Tackle the River Circuit trail for superb lookout views of the peak the Kuku Yalanji call Manjal Dimbi, meaning mountain holding back. The rock represents Kubirri who forever protects the people by confining the evil spirit Wurrumbu to The Bluff high above Mossman River. Across the Rex Creek suspension bridge, the longer Rainforest Circuit will inspire solitude-seekers chasing more distant pools (2.4km/45 minutes return).

MAKE THE TRIP

Mossman Gorge is located 80km north of Cairns (20km from Port Douglas). Park your car at the Mossman Gorge Centre and ride a shuttle bus into the gorge (every 15 minutes, 8am to 6pm). There is a café, art gallery and toilets on site (**mossmangorge.com.au**).

PORT DOUGLAS & DAINTREE
Daintree River

DAINTREE RIVER
Eyeball the predator at the top of Australia's food chain.

The late, great croc wrangler-turned-conservationist Malcolm Douglas gave me some sage advice before he passed away back in 2010. "It's not the croc you can see that you need to worry about," he warned, "it's the one you can't see that will get you."

His words have stuck with me ever since, fanning my fascination with the north's most prehistoric hunter. With an 85 million-year-old heritage, estuarine crocodiles are one of the greatest evolutionary survivors, found in rivers, creeks and lagoons right across tropical north Queensland. They can reach islands and cays more than 100km from the coast, so knowing where to swim and where to stay in the boat is vital when exploring around Cairns.

If croc spotting is on your bucket list, head for the 140km-long Daintree River where estuarine crocodiles haul out at low tide to warm themselves on the sunny mud banks. In the cool morning hours, you'll spot lots of birdlife too, so my top tip is to book your boat ahead of time and get an early start.

SPOT A CROC

Daintree River is located 110km north of Cairns. For hour-long river cruises, try Daintree River Cruise Centre, Bruce Belcher's Daintree River Cruises or Crocodile Express.

@connectingthevines

PORT DOUGLAS & DAINTREE
Daintree National Park

DAINTREE NATIONAL PARK

Walk through Australia's best, World Heritage-listed rainforest.

A discontinuous coastal wilderness that stretches from Mossman to the Bloomfield River, Daintree National Park protects some of the last Gondwanan rainforests left on the planet. It's renowned globally as a 'Living Ark', harbouring nearly all of the 19 most primitive plants still alive on earth, and a bewildering number of plant species and animals found nowhere else. Only in the Daintree might you glimpse a Thornton Peak melomys or the Bennetts tree-kangaroo, the Daintree River ringtail possum or the spotted-tailed quoll.

The Daintree's scenery is as distinctive as its inhabitants. On these traditional lands of the Eastern Kuku Yalanji people, lush, tropical rainforests rise over steep mountain ranges, and the clear creeks and rivers that drain from their summits feed coastal mangroves and swamps that spill onto long, white-sand beaches.

Much of the Daintree remains impenetrable to all but the precious creatures it protects, but its coastal fringe is studded with secluded swimming holes, walking trails and national park picnic and camping areas.

Across the Daintree River, a skinny road snakes north to Cape

PORT DOUGLAS & DAINTREE
Daintree National Park

Tribulation through misty, mountain-clad forests and across dazzling, aquamarine streams. Where this 35km-long drive curls irresistibly close to the shore, you can't help but pull over to get some sand between your toes on sweeping arcs of bleached white, palm-fringed sand.

Against the Daintree's breathtaking backdrops, a southern cassowary might suddenly appear to pluck bright blue quandongs from the forest floor before ushering its young back into the rainforest. Plunge into a croc-free waterhole, climb to the very top of the canopy, camp on a tropical beach, spotlight quolls after dark and linger for at least a few nights in one of the oldest world heritage-listed rainforests on earth.

When I was an angst-filled teenager, I dreamed of escaping to the Daintree to build a treehouse and live like a castaway on the edge of the sea. It was a fantasy that endured well into my twenties, and I pestered real estate agents with offers on rustic bungalows and wild, walk-in blocks at Cow Bay. Eventually, I bought a sailboat and took my itchy feet to sea, cruising the Daintree's reef-fringed coastline from Cairns to Cape York and back again. Buying a patch of Daintree paradise remains part of my retirement plan, just as long as its pockets of pristine wilderness can continue to hold out against the the markedly more civilised style of life south of the Daintree River.

✅ MY TOP 5

There are a bewildering number of ways to explore what rates as one of the most biologically diverse national parks in the world, so tick off this top 5 and add your own favourites too:

- [ ] 1. Climb the Daintree Discovery Centre's 23m-high canopy tower.
- [ ] 2. Devour some soursop ice cream (and jackfruit, wattleseed and chocolate pudding fruit - aka black sapote - too) at Daintree Ice Cream.
- [ ] 3. Crack a coconut on the beach at Cow Bay.
- [ ] 4. Float in the clothing-optional pools upstream of the Bloomfield Track crossing on Emmagen Creek.
- [ ] 5. Taste tropical fruits on a tour of Cape Trib Farm.

📍 MAKE THE TRIP

The Cape Tribulation section of Daintree National Park stretches from the Daintree River (110km north of Cairns) to the edge of the Bloomfield River. Allow plenty of time to explore and if you are camping, book a stay at Noah Beach campground, 8km south of Cape Tribulation.

CAMP AT: Noah Beach, 8km south of Cape Tribulation for access straight onto the sand.
SWIM AT: Woobadda Creek on the Bloomfield Track, Emmagen Creek's clothing-optional pools, or the waterholes at Mason's Store.
WATCH SUNRISE AT: Myall Beach.

69

MARRDJA BOTANICAL WALK

Step back in time on this classic Daintree stroll.

An epicentre of evolution, Daintree National Park shelters some of the oldest rainforests on earth, and 30 minutes on the Marrdja Botanical Walk is all you need to experience this extraordinary patch of World Heritage-listed wilderness. Signposted between Thornton Beach and Cape Tribulation, the boardwalk winds beneath monstrous cannonball mangroves and arcing strangler figs to reach a viewing platform over Noah Creek.

There are fiddler crabs and mudskippers to spot, and above the towering fan palms, vast sprays of colourful orchids and epiphytes stud the canopy. Marrdja's easy boardwalk is accessible to all, and at 1.2km, might occupy you for around 30 to 45 minutes.

PORT DOUGLAS & DAINTREE
Marrdja Botanical Walk

☑ TREK MY TOP 5

☐ 1. Spot cassowaries on the Jindalba trail, signposted off Cape Tribulation Road near the Daintree Discovery Centre (650m, 45 minutes return).

☐ 2. Follow bright blue Ulysses butterflies along the Kulki boardwalk for an unforgettable Cape Tribulation sunrise (600m return, easy).

☐ 3. Beachcomb south along Thornton Beach to the croccy mouth of Cooper Creek for moody views of Wundu (Thorntons Peak), the wettest peak in Australia.

☐ 4. Plant the first footprints of the day on Myall Beach (from Kulki car park, 60mins one way).

☐ 5. Tackle the Daintree's toughest trail: the steep summit climb up Mount Sorrow (7km/6hrs return).

PORT DOUGLAS & DAINTREE
Cape Tribulation

CAPE TRIBULATION
Discover the rugged coastline that snagged Cook's voyage.

Its offshore reefs may have wreaked havoc for Captain Cook, holing the Endeavour back in 1770 and sending it limping north to Cooktown, but Cape Tribulation has been making forest-lovers smile ever since. Shadowed by misty mountains and protecting world heritage-listed crocodile and cassowary habitat, Cape Tribulation severs two stellar sweeps of sand.

Park your car on Cape Trib's wild, palm-fringed shores and follow the Kulki Walk to the beach to wander north in search of your own patch of squeaky white sand. When the tide retreats, rock-hop around the corner to discover a lonelier curl of sand on beautiful Emmagen Beach before retracing your steps (10km, 2 hours return).

Few travellers tackle the short, steep trail that climbs up onto Cape Tribulation itself. It crosses the rainforested saddle before scrambling down onto magical Myall Beach. It's well-marked, and iridescent Ulysses butterflies will lead the way. From Myall Beach, you can wander endlessly south then dive back into the rainforest along the Dubuji Boardwalk. Make a break for Myall Beach at dawn to plant the day's first footsteps on the sand.

GET YOURSELF THERE

Drive 110km north of Cairns, cross the Daintree River by ferry (open 6am to midnight) and continue 35km to Cape Tribulation. The closest campsites at Noah Beach are particularly scenic (8km south), or try Cape Trib Camping for some jungle luxury, a bar and wood-fired pizza (**capetribcamping.com.au**).

THE BLOOMFIELD TRACK

4WD into the heart of the Daintree and discover her best-kept secrets.

This is an off-road adventure through one of the last bastions of remote tropical wilderness in the north. It takes you to the edge of crystalline streams and dark, croccy rivers, into secret, palm-fringed camps you can only reach on foot, and to a thunderous waterfall at the head of the Bloomfield River.

The track begins at Emmagen Creek, 5km north of Cape Tribulation, and technically ends on the other side of the Bloomfield River. But the adventure continues past Weary Bay and Wallaby Creek, to the Lions Den Hotel (for a cold beer or two). Then, after a swim at Annan Gorge, it puts you at the foot of mysterious Black Mountain on the outskirts of Cooktown. Parts of the track are so steep, concrete has been laid so that vehicles don't skid off the track trying to get through it.

THE BATTLE OF THE BLOOMFIELD

On December 1st, 1983, the Daintree Blockade hit the headlines when 60 local protestors set out to save the rainforest. They chained themselves to the treetops and buried themselves up to their necks in the path of bulldozers, generating Australia-wide support. But what began as a peaceful protest rapidly escalated into a full-scale clash with police and road workers hell-bent on clearing of a path from Cape Tribulation north to Cooktown. And when the Hawke federal government, who had already stopped the damming of Tasmania's Franklin River, failed to intervene, Queensland Premier Joh Bjelke-Petersen got his road. In August 1984, the rugged Bloomfield Track was cleared, its route largely determined from the seat of a bulldozer. The battle may have been lost, but those Daintree conservationists won the war when, four years later, the Wet Tropics of Queensland was declared a World Heritage Area.

PORT DOUGLAS & DAINTREE
The Bloomfield Track

The first time I battled the Bloomfield was by mountain bike, and those heart-stopping hill climbs aside, that trip rates as one of the best adventures I've ever had. I've tackled the trip since in air-conditioned comfort and found the journey to be no less rewarding. When you go, don't rush. Allow at least one night in Ayton or at Home Rule Rainforest Lodge on Wallaby Creek to let the Bloomfield get under your skin.

NEED IDEAS?

1. Plunge into croc-free Woobadda Creek.
2. Stroll the sands of coconut-fringed Cowie Beach.
3. Rock-hop to Bloomfield Falls, spectacular just after the wet season.
4. Catch a barra on the Bloomfield (4WD 2km south of Weary Bay to reach the river mouth).
5. Float beneath Home Rule Falls.
6. Hike to remote Cedar Bay.
7. Drink a beer at the Lions Den.
8. Swim upstream of Annan Gorge.

TAKE ON THE BLOOMFIELD

Depending on how recently the graders have been through, the Bloomfield Track might be dusty and corrugated or washed out and greasy. Towing a caravan is not advised. Check road conditions at **cook.qld.gov.au**.

PORT DOUGLAS & DAINTREE
Bloomfield Falls

BLOOMFIELD FALLS

Rock-hop to the roaring Bloomfield Falls.

Thundering 40 metres over the rugged face of Bloomfield Falls, a wet season's worth of water tumbles towards the Coral Sea, creating a dramatic whitewater flurry that's worth timing your trip to this remote community for.

Of all the sacred waterfalls around Wujal Wujal, Bloomfield Falls is the only one you can reach unguided. It's just a short scramble over the rocks from the car park to the viewing area upstream. Local custodians, the Kuku (Goo-goo) Yalanji (Ya-lan-gee), can show you others around the community at Wujal Wujal, whose name literally means 'falls'..

◉ MAKE IT HAPPEN

Bloomfield Falls is located at Wujal Wujal, 70km south of Cooktown on the sealed Bloomfield Road (or 32km north of Cape Tribulation via the unsealed Bloomfield Track). When you go, stop at the Bana Yirriji Art and Cultural Centre, open Monday to Thursday 9-4 and Friday mornings (**wujalwujalartcentre.com.au**).

⚠ TOP TIPS

Be prepared: the walk is graded strenuous. Wear a long-sleeved shirt and pants to protect against lawyer cane and leeches. Be aware that marine stingers inhabit the water from October to May (never swim) and saltwater crocodiles may dwell in estuaries. Avoid crossing tidal creeks at high tide and never swim in them.

PORT DOUGLAS & DAINTREE
Cedar Bay

CEDAR BAY
Strap on a pack and hike your way to paradise.

Hidden away in one of the most remote rainforests in the north, this coconut-fringed lagoon is blissfully deserted and utterly pristine. Rare Bennetts tree-kangaroos and southern cassowaries range the misty flanks above Cedar Bay, and so very few people plant their feet on its curl of sun-bleached sand, you'll feel like the last person on earth.

It's the same tropical utopia that attracted the attention of Queensland Police in August 1976. They destroyed Cedar Bay's harmless hippy commune and arrested its 12 residents in a shambolic drug raid that cost an estimated $65,000 and netted very little contraband in return. The hippies have long gone, but the tropical utopia still exists.

The hitch is that unless you boat in from the Bloomfield River, it takes around eight hours to hike the trail to the bay, reserving it for the most determined of solitude seekers. This is by far my favourite hiking adventure in the tropics. It begins at Homerule Rainforest Lodge, climbing beneath fan palms and tree ferns, across Granite Creek to Black Snake Rocks, and past old tin mines scattered trackside.

I've spotted Bennetts tree-kangaroos on this stretch so keep an eye out. Just beyond Ashwell Creek lies the long-deserted camp of Cedar Bay Bill, aka William Yale Evans, a hermit tin miner whose nautilus shell-covered monument overlooks Cedar Bay.

📍 LIVE THE DREAM

Cedar Bay is located in the Mangkalba section of Ngalba Bulal National Park. The trail begins at Homerule Rainforest Lodge, signposted off Bloomfield Road, 53km south of Cooktown. Allow a full day to reach Cedar Bay (BYO camping gear, food, fuel stove, first aid kit, and collect water as you cross Ashwell Creek and take away all rubbish).

77

PORT DOUGLAS & DAINTREE
Home Rule Falls

HOME RULE FALLS

Snorkel, swim, paddle and float along the Bloomfield Track's most magical waterway.

Beneath the hazy flanks of Mount Finlay, Wallaby Creek cascades untouched over Home Rule Falls. It thunders into tiers of whirlpooling cauldrons and drops through narrow chutes to rush away into the World Heritage-listed rainforest.

Pristine and impossibly clear, the creek finally slows to fill deep, wide pools, and twists and tunnels through a lush forest canopy past the shady waterfront camps at Homerule Rainforest Lodge. Set up camp on the water's edge and grab a tyre tube, paddle a canoe or don a snorkel to drift in the current along Wallaby Creek in some of the clearest water on earth.

When you can bear to tear yourself away from the creek, tackle the 40-minute walk to multi-tiered Home Rule Falls. It's a pretty rainforest stroll, and just as you begin to feel the humidity, invigorating spa pools appear beneath the falls' rugged rockface so you can throw yourself in.

GET YOURSELF THERE

Homerule Rainforest Lodge is located in Rossville, 53km south of Cooktown and is a top place to stay if you are travelling the Bloomfield Track (see page 73). Book at **homerule.com.au** and don't miss the Wallaby Creek Festival (September, **wallabycreekfestival.org.au**).

LIONS DEN HOTEL

Discover the north's quirkiest watering hole.

Did you hear the one about a woman who walks into the Lions Den, sits down for one beer and a good time later, checks in the night? Well, that woman was me, and I'll go ahead and blame the great storytelling that takes place when travellers and locals get together over brews at the quirkiest pub in TNQ.

Testament to the fact that I'm not the only traveller who's been waylaid by the chilly ales and good company, the Lions Den has stilted safari tents and a big camping area out the back. It's kid- and dog-friendly, and there's a top waterhole for safe swimming too.

Built in 1875 and slung with the kind of funky, far northern memorabilia that hallmarks every great Outback pub, the Lions Den is unique in these parts and a quirky place to overnight. Stop by for a drink but expect the unexpected: there are more tales swapped here than on all the kangaroos in Queensland.

SINK A COLDIE

The Lions Den is 28km out of Cooktown, just off the Mulligan Highway on Bloomfield Road. Find out more at **lionsdenhotel.net**.

TAKE A DIP

LITTLE ANNAN RIVER GORGE
Just behind the pub, you can swim with jungle perch and penny turtles in the sandy pools above Annan Gorge. Or rock-hop downstream to where a narrow rock chute squeezes the Little Annan River into a flurry of white water that drops 10 metres over the falls.

COOKTOWN AND CAPE YORK

Adventurous Aussies will tell you that Cooktown is where every great road trip begins, with Cape York beckoning you out of town into a remote and rugged wilderness that ends at the very tip of the country. From Cooktown north to Frangipani Bay, you'll discover blissfully remote bush campsites, impossibly clear rainforest streams, bulldust and barramundi, and unearth the rich history of the north's Indigenous peoples and the pioneering explorers who followed.

There's nothing quite like tackling a Cape York adventure, especially if you're the one behind the wheel, and it's a lot easier to execute than you might think. Bring your own vehicle or rent one in Cairns, load up your off-road gear and rumble off the bitumen on the road to adventure. When you reach The Tip, breathe in the frangipani-scented sea air, then turn around and tackle the trip all over again.

Fruit Bat Falls, Old Telegraph Track – page 101

COOKTOWN AND CAPE YORK
Black Mountain (Kalkajaka) National Park

BLACK MOUNTAIN
Unravel Cooktown's biggest mystery.

The road into Cooktown rises over giant granite tors: an odd and ominous jumble of black, balancing boulders known as Kalkajaka, the place of the spear. To the Kuku Bididji, this is where curious souls are lost forever, vanishing into the labyrinth of eerie dark passages and hidden chambers when they dare to set foot on Black Mountain.

From this place of magic and mystery, mournful cries and loud bangs are heard late at night, or so the storytelling goes. Recorded disappearances over the years and several Indigenous Dreamtime stories about this sacred mountain are enough to convince many Cooktown locals of the mountain's magical powers. I once found a small book devoted entirely to the subject at the Cooktown Maritime Museum.

The magic that turns men and women into myths is enough to keep most travellers at Black Mountain's roadside lookout, enjoying it from afar. That's good news for three exceptionally rare wildlife species found nowhere else on earth: the Black Mountain skink, Black Mountain boulder frog and the Black Mountain gecko.

📍 MAKE A STOP

Black Mountain (Kalkajaka) National Park is located 25km south of Cooktown on the Mulligan Highway. An informative roadside lookout provides good views over the mountain, but visitors are warned against venturing any further.

COOKTOWN AND CAPE YORK
Cooktown

COOKTOWN
Discover the town shaped by one man's misfortune.

When the HMB Endeavour struck an uncharted reef off Cape Tribulation on June 10th, 1770, Captain James Cook found himself in a desperate situation. His bold move – to drive his floundering ship into the shallows of a sheltered river mouth – not only saved his vessel and crew, but his entire Australian expedition.

Cook's crew spent seven weeks diligently repairing the ship's hull, the longest time ashore during their entire Aussie voyage. With botanical specimens collected in Cooktown, Joseph Banks and Daniel Solander introduced Australia's flora and fauna to the world, and when the ship finally departed, Cook carried with him lessons learnt from encounters with the traditional Guugu Yimithirr people. What he left behind was a remarkable historical legacy that resonates still.

Today, Cooktown memorialises Captain Cook at every turn with an eclectic trail of monuments, landmarks and one awesome annual festival. Every June on the Queen's Birthday long weekend, Cooktown locals step back in time to re-enact the arrival of their most famous visitor and celebrate with a three-day festival of Indigenous dance and workshops, fairs, markets, street parades and fireworks.

📍 GET YOURSELF THERE

Cooktown is located 331km north of Cairns via the inland Mulligan Highway, or 250km from Cairns via the 4WD-only Bloomfield Track (see page 73). Book festival tickets at **cooktowndiscovery.com.au** and plan your stay at **cooktownandcapeyork.com**.

COOKTOWN AND CAPE YORK
Endeavour River Fishing

ENDEAVOUR RIVER FISHING

Catch a barramundi on Cook's own river.

It is the only Australian river Captain James Cook ever named, remembered for the ship it saved after the HMS Endeavour hit a reef off Cape Tribulation. Today, the Endeavour River is revered as a haven for big, fat mud crabs and for the barramundi caught in good numbers up the river's North Arm.

You can launch your own boat at the ramp opposite the Seaview Hotel, or at the Marton boat ramp, 10 minutes north of town. Expect catches of barramundi, mangrove jack, golden trevally and fingermark, and you can spot estuarine crocodiles up North Arm on low tides from June to August.

If you haven't got a boat in tow, cast a line off the town jetty for queenfish and the occasional Spanish mackerel too. Or join a local charter upriver or to Dawson Reef just off Cooktown. If the fishing fails, order some fresh with hot chips from Gilled & Gutted or Cook's Landing Kiosk on the foreshore, and share your feed with the seagulls that gather down by the jetty right about sunset.

CHASE YOUR CATCH

Cooktown is custom-made for angling with a sealed boat ramp, jetty and a local fishing store just opposite for last-minute supplies. For boat trips and fishing tips, head to cooktownandcapeyork.com.

COOKTOWN AND CAPE YORK
Grassy Hill Lighthouse

GRASSY HILL LIGHTHOUSE

For endless Coral Sea vistas, spiced with a little Aussie history.

Drive or climb to the top of Cooktown's most famous landmark and enjoy extraordinary vistas of the winding Endeavour River and the Coral Sea. If you reach the top in time for sunrise, when the day's first light illuminates the reef, you can gaze out – as Cook often did back in 1770 – to search for a way through the treacherous patchwork of the rock, reef and sand beyond.

After the sun rises (especially if you've hiked to the top) you can follow a walking trail down the hill to secluded Cherry Tree Bay to cool off with a clothing-optional dip. Otherwise, spend a day following in Captain Cook's footsteps on a walking tour of town.

There's Cook's bronze statue to check out on the main street, Cook's cairn, and a cannon, originally installed in 1885 to thwart the threat of a Russian Invasion, which is now dramatically fired during the town's annual re-enactment of Cook's 1770 arrival.

As the day warms up, retreat to the James Cook Museum where Cook's original anchor takes pride of place in the foyer. Here, there are two storeys of artefacts that help history fall into place.

🛈 TRUE STORY

Captain James Cook was never officially a 'Captain'. He was a Lieutenant when he circumnavigated Australia, and upon return to England, was promoted to Commander, and the higher rank of Post-Captain. Only informally, as boss of the HMS Endeavour, was he rightly called 'Captain'.

COOKTOWN AND CAPE YORK
Mount Cook

MOUNT COOK
Stand on the shoulders of Cook's Mountain.

A trek to the summit of Mount Cook (431m) offers the best views in Cooktown, elevating you high above the colourful tapestry of coral reefs and sandbanks that snagged Captain Cook back in 1770. The trail is scenic too, and at 3km return, not too taxing. You'll stroll past granite boulders and through grasslands, rainforest and tropical woodland to reach a rare, accessible high point on this stretch of coast.

If you hit the trail early, before the day warms up, you might spot a northern quoll or a brilliantly coloured amethystine python on the move. The walk takes around 3-4 hours and there are no facilities, so carry water. Captain Cook first named the mountain Mount Gores to recognise his third lieutenant aboard the HMS Endeavour, but when Phillip Parker King sailed past in 1819, he renamed it Mount Cook, and this time, the name stuck.

⚲ TAKE A WALK

To reach Mount Cook National Park, follow the signs from town to the trailhead on Hannan Street. Or hike there from nearby Finch Bay (1.2km). Find out more at **parks.des.qld.gov.au**.

COOKTOWN AND CAPE YORK
Mary Watson's Grave

MARY WATSON'S GRAVE

Uncover the truth behind Cooktown's most tragic colonial saga.

In the Cooktown Cemetery, a small plaque memorialises 23-year-old Mary Watson who fled an Indigenous attack on Lizard Island in 1881. She set to sea in a beche-de-mer (sea cucumber) boiling-down-tank with her baby, Ferrier and Chinese servant, Ah Sam.

At the time, Mary's husband, Robert, was away on a six-week-long fishing trip. After drifting for nine days at sea, Mary, Ah Sam and baby Ferrier reached Watson's Island in the Howick Group, but with no water to be found, all three perished from thirst.

The story of Mary Watson's heroic struggle to survive endures, but the flipside to this tale is what caused the attack in the first place. Myth and misunderstanding abound, but Indigenous descendants of those who were killed to avenge Mary Watson, point to the sacred ground on which the Watson's fishing operation stood.

There is evidence – including a sacred Indigenous rock site at the summit of Cook Lookout – to suggest that Lizard Island was a place of initiation. At the very least, it was an important hunting ground long before the Watsons' arrival.

❗ QUENCH YOUR CURIOSITY

If this saga piques your interest, visit Cooktown's James Cook Museum which houses, amongst other things, a tiny egg cup belonging to Mary Watson. Follow Cooktown's historical walking trail from Mary Watson's memorial fountain to her gravesite at the cemetery, or visit Mary Watson's crumbling ruins on Lizard Island itself.

CONNIES BEACH, CAPE FLATTERY

Get away for great angling and beach-time on Cape Flattery's shimmering blue bay.

Paperbarks and pandanus palms shade this distinctly tropical, tri-coloured scene: a strip of silky white sand, starfish in the shallows and sea eagles soaring above Spanish mackerel in the too-blue bay.

At remote Connies Beach, a sandy 120km drive north of Cooktown, travellers stake out peaceful, shady camps by the water's edge and spend time beachcombing for nautilus shells and casting lures off the oyster-encrusted rocks for mangrove jack and tricky barramundi.

The angling is heavenly, and this spot will always be remembered as the spot where my partner (and this book's photographer) Dave reeled in his enormous 122cm-long Spanish mackerel – on a hand line no less! This catch gave rise to what is still our favourite fish meal: Cape Flattery Spanish Mackerel, marinaded with lime, chilli, coriander, garlic and fish sauce, pan-fried over hot coals and teamed with a fresh mango salad. Divine!

Campfires at Cape Flattery are de rigueur, and there's plenty of driftwood to gather. With no fees, time limits or facilities, Connies Beach is custom-made for self-sufficient travellers. Arrive with rods and books and deep pockets for all the shells you'll collect. Don't miss an early morning hike up Cape Flattery's headland for Coral Sea views of distant Lizard Island.

📍 MAKE YOUR ESCAPE

From Cooktown follow Battle Camp Road to Starcke Homestead, beach drive for 20km to Cape Flattery Silica Mine (you'll need a low tide) and continue to the north side of the cape. 4WD vehicles need to be well equipped and carry ample supplies, including drinking water and recovery gear (there is mobile phone coverage). The presence of estuarine crocodiles means no swimming.

❗ THE WORLD'S FINEST

Named by Captain James Cook, Cape Flattery's rich mineral sands are undisputedly the world's purest.

COOKTOWN AND CAPE YORK
Quinkan Reserve Ancient Rock Art

QUINKAN ROCK ART GALLERY
Meet the magical spirits who inhabit Split Rock.

UNESCO rated this one of the world's top 10 rock art galleries: 13,000-year-old ochre paintings of the mesmerising sorcerers and Quinkan spirits who inhabit Split Rock's towering sandstone bluff.

This is easily Cape York's most accessible rock art, and the most impressive you are likely to lay eyes upon without initiation. Located right by the roadside, 12km south of Laura, Split Rock's storytelling is painted on overhung rock faces within easy reach of walkers.

My favourite is the Tall Spirits Gallery – where six thin, friendly Quinkans will mesmerise you. This distinctive rock art is quite unlike anything I've seen elsewhere in Australia.

Split Rock's self-guided walking trail leads along the base of the escarpment where the Quinkan galleries are located, then climbs to the top of Turtle Rock for expansive vistas. As you cross the escarpment, spot the Indigenous earth ovens carved into termite mounds before descending into the magnificent maze of rock outcrops and caves that showcase the elaborate Guguyalangi Gallery, the largest and most complex collection of art at Split Rock.

Here, miniature paint-blown hands crowd a multitude of lofty overhangs, and magical male and female figures point to sorcery at this spot. Beyond Guguyalangi Gallery, the car park is within easy reach, and a full 4km loop takes around 2.5 hours (carry drinking water).

SEE SPLIT ROCK

Split Rock is signposted off the Peninsula Development Road, 12km south of Laura (entry by $5 donation, payable at Laura's Quinkan Cultural Centre). Other sites in the Quinkan Reserve are accessible only by guided tour (see **quinkancc.com.au** for details). Spend a night in Laura or continue 27km north to camp in Rinyirru (Lakefield) National Park.

COOKTOWN AND CAPE YORK
Rinyirru (Lakefield) National Park

RINYIRRU (LAKEFIELD) NATIONAL PARK

Camp, fish and 4WD to the faraway edge of Princess Charlotte Bay.

Some of Cape York's most adventurous camping, rough off-roading and off-the-scale fishing takes place in remote Rinyirru (Lakefield) National Park (CYPAL). This is Queensland's second-largest national park – 542,000 hectares in all – so expect

COOKTOWN AND CAPE YORK
Rinyirru (Lakefield) National Park

plenty of elbowroom and a bewildering choice of 25 waterfront camps on barramundi-filled lagoons and rivers that drain away into Princess Charlotte Bay.

There's birdlife and crocodiles in equal abundance, and although there's barely a toilet to be found, Cape York anglers and wildlife watchers can't get enough of this place. You could lose yourself for weeks at Rinyirru, but if your itinerary isn't that loose, drive 30 minutes out of Laura to Old Laura Homestead to marvel at the stunning lotus lilies on Red Lily Lagoon or fish for barramundi in the Laura River.

Remarkably intact, the oldest part of Old Laura Homestead dates back to 1892 when Peter MacDermott and Fergus O'Beirne felled local Leichhardt trees to build its walls. They laid its floors of ox-blood clay from termite mounds, dampened daily with ash and water. There are basic bush campsites on the Laura River nearby, but if you haven't shaken off your daily shower ritual, head back to Laura for the night.

Tracks from the homestead push north past lily-covered lagoons to Catfish Waterhole where you can spot crocodiles, birds and turtles. There's a top camp at Kalpower Crossing (the only one in the park with cold showers, toilets, and taps), and more good camping at the Hahn River crossing. For access to Princess Charlotte Bay (PCB), head to the Bizant River boat ramp. There are dugong, dolphins and turtles to spot on PCB, and I can personally vouch for the top angling and wildlife watching up the Kennedy, Bizant, Normanby and Marrett Rivers.

📍 TAKE THIS TRIP

Allow around three hours to reach the national park from Cooktown via the often rough Battlecamp Road and a swim at Isabella Falls, or travel 17km from Laura. The park opens June 1st, weather permitting (northern camps open one month later), and has only limited facilities (generators and fires allowed). Be aware that there is no mobile phone coverage in the park beyond the New Laura ranger base.

FLINDERS ISLAND GROUP

Discover fantastic fishing and sacred Yindayin rock art on faraway Flinders Island.

Cast away in the Owen Channel, we watch a dugong surface slowly to snatch a breath before diving down to groom the lush seagrass beneath our boat. Enormous green sea turtles float past too, ignoring us and our yacht as we reel in catches of queenfish and mackerel, golden trevally and delicious, flowery rock cod.

The Flinders' bewitching group of eight sandstone islands rates as one of my favourite sailing destinations and the fishing is utterly, unbelievably good. Dugongs

COOKTOWN AND CAPE YORK
Flinders Island Group

and sea turtles are spotted in great numbers, lured by the highest diversity of seagrass found anywhere on Queensland's east coast. The sandstone lookouts and rugged, shell-strewn beaches are a castaway's dream, and best of all, it's accessible to any traveller with a tinny via Bathurst Heads on southern Cape York.

The island's blue, coral-fringed lagoons might even be idyllic if they weren't home to enormous estuarine crocodiles as well.

Crocodile slide marks are everywhere, so with swimming off the itinerary, I spend time here by hiking Yindayin (Stanley) Island instead. Here you can explore outstanding rock art shelters and climb to windows in the sandstone high on Toombiembui Rock for extraordinary, bird's-eye views.

The Aba Yalgayi saltwater people, who fished, camped, painted and were buried on the islands, have left behind an incredible heritage and their Yindayin rock shelters, middens and artefacts are some of the best on Cape York. You'll spot shell middens near the Fredrick Point campground on Flinders Island, and a walk alongside Aapa Spit reveals four unmarked graves, old wells, hut sites and the rock famously autographed by the crew of the HMS Dart back in 1899.

📍 PLAN YOUR ESCAPE

Flinders Island is located 11km off Bathurst Heads and is accessible via Rinyirru (Lakefield) National Park. The rustic Fredrick Point campground on Flinders Island provides rainwater tanks and a picnic shelter (BYO camping gear). Visit during the winter dry season (June to October), book campsites (**parks.des.qld.gov.au**) and check the weather in advance (**bom.gov.au**).

MUSGRAVE ROADHOUSE

Spend a night at this old Overland Telegraph Station.

Whether it's for the cold beers or to trade tales with fellow Cape York off-roaders, Musgrave Roadhouse is a popular rest stop, nestled mid-way to The Tip at the foot of the Bamboo Range. But this historical spot has stories to tell too, and it all begins with the old telegraph pole that stands sentry over the roadhouse.

Back in 1887 when the Overland Telegraph Line was strung out from Cooktown to The Tip, Musgrave was established as a repeater station along a route that explorer J.R. Bradford scouted out in a record three-month blitz. Once word got out about Cape York's booming potential, Musgrave became a rest stop for explorers and entrepreneurs.

John Augustus Mayers was one of them – a major shareholder in Coen's Great Northern Goldmine – who died at the Musgrave Telegraph Station in 1924 and now rests under the old mango tree out front. Later, Musgrave became a cattle run and roadhouse too, and today it welcomes travellers off the track with a grassy camp, rooms, fuel, meals and cold ales.

If you've got your eyes on the scenery as you travel Cape York, you'll notice that Musgrave Roadhouse sits between two distinctly different landscapes. To the south, the road dips to milky streams and lily-covered, paperbark lagoons, while on higher, drier ground, spindly gums, grass trees and termite mounds stud the landscape. Beyond Musgrave where the road climbs the Bamboo Range to an elevation of 270m, creamy clay replaces the ubiquitous red dirt and fern-leafed grevilleas fringe a verdant landscape rejuvenated by wet season rains.

SPEND A NIGHT

Musgrave Roadhouse is located 135km north of Laura. It has a basic motel and simple campsites out the back. It's open April to December. **(musgraveroadhouse.com.au)**.

COOKTOWN AND CAPE YORK
The Bend, Coen

THE BEND, COEN

Catch yourself a feed of wild cherabin in these clear, rainforested pools.

Park your 4WD at the water's edge and spend a day wading and swimming far upstream to throw yourself into all the deeply relaxing pools scattered along the Coen River. Retreat afterwards to shake out your camp chairs, stoke a starry-night campfire and watch sulphur-crested cockatoos screeching from the treetops. In the morning, collect tasty freshwater cherabin from your yabby pot for the ultimate Cape York breakfast.

This shady bend in the Coen River is a breezy, standout spot for Cape York pilgrims: spacious and grassy, and free of fees and time limits so you can settle in and relax. Use it as a base to explore Coen, 3km to the south, or for adventures into nearby Oyala Thumotang National Park (CYPAL) – a rugged, remote patch of wilderness accessed 25km north of here.

The Bend supplies all the really essential facilities – a toilet, rubbish bins and fireplaces. If you need power, Coen's Exchange Hotel offers riverside sites, hot meals and cold ales.

TOP TIP

Just north of Coen, a Queensland quarantine station stops travellers returning from the north, so have all your fruit and vegetables ready for inspection.

GET YOURSELF THERE

The Bend is located 3km north of Coen on the Peninsula Development Road. Camping is free, pet-friendly and generators are permitted. Nearby Coen supplies basic groceries, fuel and drinking water.

WEIPA
Stay and play on Albatross Bay and unearth Weipa's rich Indigenous heritage.

Locals say the barramundi flows on tap at this anglers' paradise on the Gulf of Carpentaria, renowned for its big rivers and endless sea views. But if you don't know a trout from a trevally, there's exceptional Indigenous history to unearth. On the northern bank of the Mission River at Red Beach (Prunung), 400-year-old cockle shell middens are piled high, some of the largest in the world.

Here too stands a display of

COOKTOWN AND CAPE YORK
Weipa

scarred sugarbag trees holed by Indigenous Australians to collect native bee honey. They were relocated in 2007 off Rio Tinto's mining lease. On the waterfront at Evans Landing, I love to wander around Weipa's Western Cape Cultural Centre – a fascinating little find with free entry – and afterwards, line up with the locals down on the wharf to lure the passing parade of queenfish, trevally and grunter.

Few travellers arrive in Weipa without a tinny in tow, but you can hire one once you arrive and launch it at Rocky Point or Evans Landing to head up the Mission, Embley or Hey Rivers. If the crocs have had their fill, there's an outstanding smorgasbord of fish up for grabs: salmon, trevally, grunter, fingermark, jewfish and more.

Try fishing off the points to hook up trout, mackerel or cobia. Or drive 86km north to Mapoon's Port Musgrave and launch your boat into more remote waters off Cullen Point or Cloughs Landing.

Angler or not, everyone gathers on the sand at day's end to watch the sun light up the Gulf as it sets across Albatross Bay. Find your own patch of sand to watch the stunning sunset show, or sip your sundowners at Albatross Bay Resort, or mingle with miners at Weipa's local bowls and golf clubs.

TRUE STORY

North of Weipa on the Pennefather River, the first recorded contact between Indigenous Australians and Europeans took place in 1606 when Dutchman Willem Janszoon sailed the Duyfken within sight of the Yupangati people.

MAKE IT HAPPEN

Weipa is located 510km north of Laura via mostly sealed roads. Weipa Caravan Park on Albatross Bay offers the only campsites in town so book ahead (campweipa.com.au). Time your trip to catch the Weipa Fishing Classic in June or Weipa's Bull Ride in August, considered one of the best on the Cape.

CHILLI BEACH

Chill out on Cape York's most iconic, coconut-fringed beach.

This idyllic swathe of sand in Kutini Payamu (Iron Range) National Park (CYPAL) is one of the most beautiful on the Cape, and with just 25 campsites on offer, wild and windswept Chilli Beach books out fast. The southeasterly winds that bend the coconut palms over the winter months do little to deter adventurous travellers who arrive fully laden for long beach stays and angling sessions.

The fierce breezes that blow might account for its name, but Chilli Beach is a sunny spot that nudges against a blissful arc of bright blue. A verdant fringe of palms drops coconuts onto a startling white sand beach, and the views, the beachcombing and the isolation is sheer heaven.

MAKE IT YOURS

To get there, head north of Archer River Roadhouse and take the track to Portland Roads, or follow the rugged Frenchmans Track if you are up for an adventure. Facilities are limited to toilets (no generators, 21-day stay limit), and there is limited phone coverage on Chilli Beach itself. Book your campsite well in advance.

COOKTOWN AND CAPE YORK
The Old Telegraph Track

THE OLD TELEGRAPH TRACK
Take up Cape York's toughest challenge.

Since the first car reached The Tip in 1928, a cavalcade of adventurers have embarked on their own extreme journeys: running, riding horses, driving lawnmowers and even pushing wheelbarrows up Cape York. As the traffic increases and more bitumen gets laid, the Old Telegraph Track – roughly 150km of Cape York's original route – endures to test the mettle of rugged off-roaders. If nothing else, it's a break from the main road's corrugations.

Not everyone wants to put their 4WD skills (or their vehicles) to the test, but this route rewards with incredible bush camping, blissful, croc-free swimming holes and some pretty Insta-worthy moments. The adventure begins at Bramwell Roadhouse Junction where you turn off the Peninsula Development Road onto the Old Telegraph Track.

DON'T MISS
Bramwell Station's Big Weekend (June/July, **bramwellstationcapeyork.com.au**).

The first challenge is one of the toughest – the steep crossing of Palm Creek – but once you conquer that, you can rest easy on the banks of the Dulhunty River to swim and camp for the night. Next up is Bertie Creek and the legendary Gunshot Creek crossing, which some lament is far easier today than it once was.

Across Gunshot, push north to Cockatoo Creek (walking your route across first), and linger for the beautiful camps and swimming before exiting onto Bamaga Road to join the Cape York convoy at Fruit Bat Falls. On the track's northern section from Bamaga Road to the Jardine River ferry, you'll discover sensational, croc-free swimming spots on Mistake and Cannibal Creeks, and tackle a deep (up to 1.5 metres) crossing of Nolan's Brook.

The track is notorious for vehicle breakdowns, expensive recoveries and damaged egos, but driven carefully and without bravado, it's very manageable for the experienced 4WDer. Plus, you can bypass the most infamous sections and still say you've tackled it. Gunshot Creek has a bypass track which detours roughly 30km, intersecting back with the Old Telegraph Track just on the northern side of Gunshot, so you can still watch the action. You can leave it early by taking

DON'T TRY IT IN A RENTAL

Rental 4WDs are generally permitted on Cape York roads, just not on the rugged Old Telegraph Track (hire yours at **4wdhirecairns.com.au**).

COOKTOWN AND CAPE YORK
The Old Telegraph Track

the west-bound track just before Mistake Creek, and so bypass the deep (usually over the bonnet) and often treacherous Nolans Brook. Here the soft, sandy bottom gets churned up after two or three 4WDs cross it, so it must be left to settle before you attempt a crossing. Have recovery gear ready.

If you don't want to risk your vehicle, you can access the track at points from the main road to watch the action at gnarly creek crossings or soak in croc-free swimming holes. Palm Creek, Gunshot and Nolans Brook are accessible via access tracks, while Sam and Mistake Creeks both have great camping. You can get to them by turning east off the Southern Bypass Road about 30km north of the Fruit Bat Falls turnoff.

📍 GO OTT

You'll need a well-equipped high clearance 4WD to cover the 150km Old Telegraph Track (from Bramwell Junction Roadhouse to the Jardine River Ferry). Allow at least three days. Time your trip during the dry season from May to September. Although it is unmaintained, you can check road conditions on Cape York at **cook.qld.gov.au**.

COOKTOWN AND CAPE YORK
Kennedy's Lost Camp

KENNEDY'S LOST CAMP

Meet Cape York's boldest explorer with a tragic tale.

He was the first European to almost make it to the Tip and, despite grit and daring, his disastrous expedition was a lesson in what not to do in TNQ.

When Kennedy set out from the Cardwell coastline in May 1848, he had no idea what he was walking into. His crew of 12 quickly floundered in mangroves swamped by wet season rains. Despite abandoning their wagons, the men struggled for 10 excruciating weeks only to find themselves far inland and just 16km north of their first camp..

Over the next seven months, eight men were lost to disease, accidents, fatigue and conflicts with Indigenous tribes. Upon reaching the Richardson Range, one man accidently shot himself. He was left in the care of two others while Kennedy and guide Jacky Jacky struggled north.

Tantalisingly close to the Tip, Kennedy was speared and died. Jacky Jacky made it to the waiting supply ship and sailed in search of the three left behind. But they were never seen again.

It's a tale that resonates with me still because adventures on Cape York are always tinged with just a little daring (and Kennedy is by far my favourite underdog explorer). If you're headed to the Tip, don't miss a stop at Kennedy's Memorial that overlooks the dense heath-covered dunes that have long since engulfed his lost camping companions.

📍 REMEMBERING KENNEDY

Les Hiddens, the Bush Tucker Man, located the site where Kennedy died back in the 1970s, but his memorial is opposite the Heathlands Ranger Base, 55km north of the old Telegraph Track junction. Camp close by on the beach at Captain Billy Landing.

COOKTOWN AND CAPE YORK
Captain Billy Landing

CAPTAIN BILLY LANDING

Camp by the sea on Captain Billy's coast.

Raw and windswept and nestled beneath towering sea cliffs, Captain Billy Landing is an outstanding coastal camp on a blissfully deserted beach that stretches endlessly north. This beach, peppered with prized nautilus shells and the nests of green sea turtles, lures beachcombers, anglers and birders who'll spot dusky honeyeaters, yellow-bellied sunbirds and rainbow bee-eaters flitting about the colourful, heath-covered dunes.

Captain Billy was an Indigenous Australian and guide who led government surveyor Dr Logan Jack to the coast on his 1879-80 Cape York expedition. Today, Captain Billy's grassy camp is national park-protected and provides a huge picnic shelter, toilets and fire pits. At first light, carry your cuppa into the high dunes north of camp to witness one final Coral Sea sunrise before the road to The Tip swings onto the western side of the Cape.

📍 SPEND A NIGHT

Drive 67km north of Bramwell Junction, take the signposted detour east and continue 27km to the beach. Book your campsite in advance before your phone signal drops out.

COOKTOWN AND CAPE YORK
Twin Falls

TWIN FALLS
Soak off the red dust in these cool, croc-free pools.

At the Twin Falls turn-off, our trouble-free journey to the Tip ended in classic Cape York style: straddling a washed-out track and taking 25 hair-raising minutes to inch our camper trailer just 8km. But our persistence paid off, and in less than half that time we had hiked to Canal Creek and thrown ourselves in: splashing across two tiers of irresistibly clear pools beneath magnificent Twin Falls.

Floating in the sandy shallows at day's end, your red, dusty feet dangling in the current, is a sublime experience in croc country where so many waterholes are off-limits. Close by, the national park campsites are spacious, bushy nooks, and short walking trails lead directly to Twin Falls and two other lovely swimming holes - the Saucepan and Eliot Falls.

This string of falls called Yaranjangu is recognised as the last traditional warring place of the Atambaya and Angkamuthi peoples. The pools stay full year-round, fed by water that seeps through sandstone bedrock to swell the Jardine, Queensland's largest perennial river.

📍 BRAVE THE TRACK

Twin (and Eliot) Falls are signposted off the Bamaga Road, 119km north of Bramwell Junction. You'll have to tackle 8km of the Old Telegraph Track, and one long, above-the-wheel-arches, creek crossing to get there. It usually has a firm bottom and isn't too hard if you keep a bow-wave of water ahead of you. The campground provides wheelchair-accessible toilets, drinking water, picnic tables and firepits (no generators). Book campsites online before arriving as there is no phone coverage on-site.

COOKTOWN AND CAPE YORK
Mutee Head

MUTEE HEAD
After bone-rattling days of corrugations, find your way to this slice of paradise.

Park your 4WD under the casuarinas, grab your fishing rods and beachcombing bags, and skip across a squeaky curl of sand to cool your heels, cast a line and watch sea turtles floating in the shallows. Perched on the edge of a bright, blue bay, the free camping areas on either side of Mutee Head are equally idyllic. Each offers an unbeatable tropical backdrop for everything you came to Cape York to do.

Cast straight off the beach at high tide or launch a tinny on Mutee Head's southern side for reliable catches of mackerel, queenies, trevally, and flathead. If you've got barra on your mind (or mangrove jack or cod), 4WD the sandy track signposted north of camp to fish and spot estuarine crocodiles at the mouth of the Jardine River.

You can beachcomb endlessly on both sides of Mutee Head, scooping up shells and all kinds of useful flotsam and jetsam washed ashore. The Mutee Head camps provide only firepits for your fish dinners, so bring plenty of drinking water. If you run out, drive 15km back along the access track to the bridge and collect (and treat) freshwater from the creek.

If there's a downside to Mutee Head it's not being able to take a real swim, so get wet at Twin, Eliot or Fruit Bat Falls before you arrive.

◉ MAKE IT YOURS

Drive 27km beyond the Jardine River ferry crossing, take the signposted turn-off to the west and continue 20km to Mutee Head (bring drinking water). Camping at selected sites on Injinoo land is included in your ferry ticket (nparc.qld.gov.au).

SEISIA
Celebrate Friday night at the Fishing Club.

A distinctly laidback vibe permeates mainland Australia's most northern community, soothing rattled off-roaders with a gorgeous curl of coastline and lots and lots of friendly Thursday-Island smiles.

Settled by a family of Saibai islanders who sailed two pearling luggers to its shores in 1948, Seisia is a tiny town with extraordinary fishing and a singularly excellent watering hole – the Fishing Club – that serves up not-to-be-missed tunes, ales and seafood dinners on Friday and Saturday nights.

Locals and travellers gather on the town jetty to fish the swift-flowing current that flows between Seisia and nearby Red Island, carrying fish close to the shore. Come at dusk to jig for squid and eat calamari for dinner, or cast lures from the jetty to catch the biggest mackerel, barramundi, fingermark and queenfish of your life. Launch a boat straight off the beach, or paddle your kayak to nearby Red Island to discover little-walked beaches and the well-preserved remains of an Indigenous fish trap.

Most visitors make use of the supermarket and facilities inland at Bamaga, which busies itself with The Tip's administrative duties, leaving sleepy Seisia to move at its own, leisurely pace.

📍 LINGER LONGER

Stay on the beach at Seisia Holiday Park, or grab supplies and push north to the scenic sites at Punsand Bay, 5km west of The Tip (**capeyorkcamping.com.au**).

COOKTOWN AND CAPE YORK
The Tip: Frangipani Bay

THE TIP
Stand at the top of Australia.

A low-lying spine of rock that touches the sea at the very tip of Australia, Mount Bremer marks the culmination of every great Cape York adventure. With views over York and Eborac Islands, The Tip is a poignant, much-photographed spot on the edge of Frangipani Bay where you can fish and camp to see the sun set and rise over the top of the country.

Tackling the hike takes just 15 minutes (and a fortnight's worth of off-road fun), and when you turn back south, you'll have a slightly shorter Bucket List. From the car park, scale the rock slabs and follow the well-worn trail north, adding pebbles to the rock pinnacles gathering height as you go.

At low tide, drop down onto Frangipani Beach, known as Pajinka, and beachcomb to its faraway end, chasing the bright blue solider crabs that scurry and spiral into the sand as you approach.

Frangipani's big, curling bay just begs to be explored, and you can camp there for free. Solitude is just about guaranteed – bar the Torresian pigeons that feed in the treetops – and every time our family has visited, we've had the tip of Australia all to ourselves.

📍 DRIVE TO THE EDGE

The corrugated road that bumps for 32km from Bamaga to Frangipani Bay (Pajinka) is often the roughest, most bone-chattering of the whole adventure north. Between the Croc Tent and The Tip, there is usually a lot of traffic, so slow down on corners and through the dense forest section as you near Pajinka. Free camp here and bring drinking water (visit **nparc.qld.gov.au** to find out more), or backtrack to the wonderful Punsand Bay where there are showers, a bar and shaded campsites (**capeyorkcamping.com.au**)

COOKTOWN AND CAPE YORK
Thursday Island

THURSDAY ISLAND

Go as far north as you can travel without your passport.

The Torres Strait's archipelago of 274 dreamy isles stretches all the way to Papua New Guinea, but the top tourist sites are concentrated on the turquoise-fringed isle that locals call TI. It's the centre of the Torres Strait's Kaurareg people, but its culture is incongruously interwoven with Worl War II and local pearling history too.

This part of the picture is unravelled with a visit to Green Hill Fort's underground Torres Strait Historical Museum. Follow it up with a trip to the local cemetery where hundreds of Japanese pearl divers are memorialised. The flipside to this is the discoveries you'll make at the extraordinary Gab Titu Cultural Centre. Its changing exhibitions showcase the rich tapestry of the region's unique, distinctive cultures with art and artefacts to view and buy. Entry is free.

Put yourself in a Seaman Dan song by sipping a chilly beer in Australia's most northerly pub, the Torres Hotel. If you have time, head for neighbouring Horn Island which has the dubious honour of being the second most bombed place in Australia, and the first attacked by the Japanese during WWII.

📍 BOOK YOUR ESCAPE

From Seisia, Peddells Ferry offers tours and transfers from Monday to Saturday in the peak season (June to September, **peddellsferry.com.au**). Alternatively, fly from Cairns direct to Horn Island with Qantas (**qantas.com**).

CASSOWARY COAST

Queensland's loftiest mountain peaks snag the clouds, channelling wet season downpours to fill the dreamy rainforest pools at their feet. Cassowaries range these misty green zones, their bright blue plumage easily spotted through the fan palm forests whose tasty fruits the cassowary adores. As you explore, iridescent blue Ulysses butterflies flit through the canopy and bandicoots forage the forest floor.

Protected as part of the Wet Tropics World Heritage Area, the Cassowary Coast stretches north from Cardwell to Cairns, sandwiched between towering granite peaks and dazzling white sand beaches. Climb to Josephine Fall's multi-tiered cascades and chill your bones in Babinda's sublime boulder-strewn waterholes. Stand on the banks of the croccy Russell River, trek the length of Hinchinbrook Island, and find your kind of thrill at Mission Beach where you can dive, SUP, sea kayak, skydive, snorkel, sail, mountain bike, river raft and finally, relax.

Harvey Creek, Misty Mountains – page 118.

CASSOWARY COAST
Babinda Boulders

BABINDA BOULDERS

Take the plunge into North Queensland's favourite waterhole.

Nestled against the rainforested slopes of Queensland's highest mountains, enormous granite boulders divert the flow of Babinda Creek into deep, translucent pools and over treacherous granite falls. Here, according to Indigenous Yidinydji tribe lore, the beautiful Oolana dwells, calling for her lost lover and beckoning visitors into this stunning Wet Tropics oasis.

Each year more than four and a half metres of rain falls on Babinda, snagged by Mount Bartle Frere's towering 1622 metre-high summit to surge through lush tropical rainforest and fill my pick of the most irresistible, croc-free waterholes in the far north.

Babinda's chilly pools are impossibly clear and perfect for snorkelling in search of freshwater turtles, jungle perch, and the eels and yabbies that hide amongst the river pebbles. There are more secluded swimming holes upstream along the Goldfield Track where bright butterflies flit through the forest. Keep your gaze skywards to spot the brilliant, electric-blue Ulysses butterfly and Australia's largest, the Cairns birdwing butterfly.

After water time, hang out with the bandicoots at Babinda's free campsite and return to stroll through the forest to Devils Pool Lookout (470m one-way) and Boulders Gorge, perfect in the quiet hours of dusk or dawn when the wild water roars and Oolana calls.

STAY A WHILE

Follow the Bruce Highway 60km south of Cairns to Babinda and continue 6km to the Boulders (free camping, coldwater showers, water, free gas barbecues, picnic shelters, toilets and a playground). Find out more at cairns.qld.gov.au.

CASSOWARY COAST
Josephine Falls

JOSEPHINE FALLS
Swim in the shadow of Queensland's highest peak.

In the forested foothills that flank Queensland's loftiest peak, the Josphine River surges and slides over its spectacular, multi-tiered falls. High above with its head in the clouds, Mt Bartle Frere casts a shadow, snagging more than 10,000mm of annual rainfall to feed the lush rainforests at its feet.

Josephine Falls is the mountain's most striking chasm with three tiers of waterholes and sheer granite slides, located an hour's drive south of Cairns in the rugged wilds of Wooroonooran National Park.

Popular with locals and travellers keen to escape the heat, Josphine Falls lures thrill-seekers too, but its slippery granite slabs and powerful flow are not to be underestimated. You can safely swim in the waterhole at its base, and wander through the lowland rainforest to three platforms that overlook the spectacular falls.

The short, sealed access path is suitable for wheelchairs and strollers (600m), but if you need something more challenging, shoulder a pack and tackle the tough mountain climb to Bartle Frere's distant, misty summit.

FIND THE FALLS

Drive 66km south of Cairns, turn west off the Bruce Highway 2km past Miriwinni and continue for 8km to Josephine Falls picnic area (**parks.des.qld.gov.au**).

STAND ON CHOOREECHILLUM

At 1622m, Mount Bartle Frere is Queensland's highest peak and the spiritual home of the Noongyanbudda Ngadjon people whose spirits dwell on the summit. You can climb the mountain in 10-12 hours (7.5km) from Josphine Falls, following an 1890s-era route taken by tin miners to reach their claim beneath the summit.

PARONELLA PARK

Conjure your inner Spaniard with a trip to this tropical castle.

José Paronella dreamed up this historical Spanish-style castle back in 1935, turning five acres of creekside rainforest into a breathtaking wonderland of moss-covered stone, waterfalls and tropical gardens. Together with wife Margarita, the pair built the castle and planted 7000 trees. They even channelled the spring-fed flow of Theresa Creek through a hydroelectric plant that continues to power Paronella Park today.

Clearly Jose and Margarita had quite a vision, and despite almost a century of cyclones, fires and floods, the castle and its gardens have endured. Visitors today still picnic by the falls and feed the snapping turtles, eels and sooty grunters. There are guided storytelling tours and a café too. If you spend the night in one of Paronella's cabins or the campground, you can join the Darkness Falls tour that literally lights up the night.

CASSOWARY COAST
Paronella Park

🛈 TOP TIP

Entry to Paronella Park includes one free night in the campground (cabins cost extra) and entry onto the Darkness Falls tour.

📍 MAKE A STOP

Paronella Park is signposted off the Bruce Highway, 120km south of Cairns, and is open from 9am to 7.30pm daily (**paronellapark.com.au**).

CASSOWARY COAST
Misty Mountains

MISTY MOUNTAINS
Follow in the footsteps of Indigenous nomads.

While scrambling up the rugged Djilgarrin Track through a prickly web of wait-a-while vine, I paused midway to pluck a few leeches and realised that the Ma:Mu and Jirrbal people had to be made of pretty tough stuff.

On seasonal wanders between the mountains and the coast, these nomadic Australians forged this ancient pathway that cuts an excruciatingly steep route up the misty foothills of the Cardwell Range. Today, bushwalkers can adventure along 130km of Indigenous foot trails and centuries-old logging tracks that together form Australia's longest network of high altitude rainforest trails.

Interconnected trails set out from Tully and Mena Creek on the coast, and Ravenshoe and Millaa Millaa on the Tablelands. Walks might occupy you from four hours to four days, and although the two-day Djilgarrin Track challenges me, it rewards with chilly river crossings, cassowary sightings and a side-trip to striking Elizabeth Grant Falls (31km return). At the top of the trail, you get to bivvy on the rocks at Walter's Waterhole before retracing your steps to Cochable Creek.

◉ HIT THE TRAILS

Misty Mountains has 130km of walking tracks to explore. The cool, dry winter months are best for hiking, to avoid the heat, march flies and leeches. Plan your hike at **parks.des.qld.gov.au**

CASSOWARY COAST
Mission Beach

MISSION BEACH
Swoon over every inch of this tricoloured coastline.

It's a laidback holiday haven with a cool beachy vibe, and the rainforest at Mission Beach really does spill onto the sand, bringing rare, endangered cassowaries in clear, close view. Beyond the swaying palm trees, the Great Barrier Reef sweeps close to the coast and Eddy Reef woos divers and snorkellers on easy day trips.

Good food lures everyone to the beachfront to ogle the island-studded vista. Everywhere, people kayak or SUP, and bike along the trails that lead deep into the forest where southern cassowaries roam.

Whether Mission Beach lives up to its reputation as the adventure capital of Australia probably depends on whether you fancy throwing yourself out of a plane, but there's no denying there are thrills aplenty. When I first moved here, a sandy campsite on Mission Beach was my happy home, and kayaking this very coastline is one of my all-time favourite adventures.

For DIY exploring, hire a SUP and paddle south to Lover's Beach at Lugger Bay, or grab a mountain bike from Mission Beach Bike Hire to tackle the Musgravea Trail in Djiru National Park (6km one-way). Take a water taxi to Dunk Island, known as Coonanglebah, meaning 'island of peace and plenty', and climb Mt Kootaloo (7km/3hrs return). Afterwards, fall into the sea off Muggy Muggy Beach for colourful, crowd-free snorkelling.

MAKE YOUR ESCAPE

Visit over the dry season (May to September). Camp by the sea at Mission Beach or Bingil Bay (**cassowarycoast.qld.gov.au**) or try the Sanctuary Retreat, a registered nature reserve with canopy cabins, yoga and wholefood menus (**sanctuaryretreat.com.au**). Reef Express offers plastic-free, reef-friendly snorkelling trips (**missionbeachislandreefadventures.com.au**).

CASSOWARY COAST
Djiru National Park

DJIRU NATIONAL PARK

Famous for its dazzling fan palms and the cassowaries they feed.

Buffering Mission Beach's coconut-fringed coastline, Djiru National Park is where you go to encounter the highest concentration of southern cassowaries in the world. These flamboyant, flightless, and very much endangered beauties range the Licuala ramsayi fan palm forests throughout Mission Beach. They feed on the fragrant fleshy fruit that falls from the Licuala's towering, two metre-wide fronds.

Their vivid green mosaic studs the high canopy, shading hikers on the Fan Palm Walk (20 mins) and bikers on the Musgravea trail (6km one-way) that cuts through Djiru National Park. The Dreaming Trail at Lacey Creek is another favourite for its serene, freshwater pools and the chance to catch cassowaries on the move at dawn (6.4km return).

FIND OUT MORE

Visit the C4 Environment Centre on Porter Promenade to learn about cassowaries and their conservation (**cassowarryconservation.asn.au**).

CASSOWARY COAST
Tully Gorge

TULLY GORGE
Ride the wildest white water in the north.

In Australia's wettest town, a whopping 7.9 metres of rain hammers down every year, so it's a given that Tully's namesake river can deliver a pumping good whitewater ride. The Tully River delivers, and its rapids – Corkscrew, Disappearing Falls and Flip Wilson – hide nothing about the kind of wild thrills that await on a rafting trip through Tully Gorge.

The Tully River's tempestuous flow might be tempered by a hydro-electricity plant upstream, but enough water is released daily to keep the rapids at grade 3-4. Experienced rafters will have a blast here, and beginners can join fully guided day trips out of Cairns.

SWIM AT ALLIGATOR'S NEST

There's magical energy at this secret spot where three swift-flowing creeks join forces, plunging through the rainforest to fill a chain of deep, rejuvenating pools. Despite its unlikely name, Alligator's Nest is a heavenly spot to swim and was once the secret meeting place for a perfectly harmless scout troop known as the "Alligators". Find it 6.5km north of Tully. BYO picnic and snorkelling gear.

RIDE THE RIVER

Tully is located 140km south of Cairns on the Bruce Highway. From town, the Cardstone-Tully Gorge Road follows the Tully River for 40km upstream to reach bushwalking trailheads, river lookouts and picnic spots. For trips, try Raging Thunder Adventures (**cairnsrafting.com.au**), RnR White Water Rafting (**raft.com.au**), Foaming Fury (**foamingfury.com.au**) or Wildside Adventures (**wildsideadventures.com.au**).

CASSOWARY COAST
Cardwell Spa Pool

CARDWELL SPA POOL
Soak away the day in this opalescent blue pool.

The wet season rains that replenish Scrubby Creek every summer send it swirling into this sparkling blue sensation, hidden in the rainforested foothills of the Cardwell Range. Tumbling into Spa Pool's tiny rock hole, the turbulent, bubbling flow leaches limestone out of the rock to colour this perfect pool an unbelievable, iridescent blue.

When I called Cardwell home, Spa Pool was little known and a favourite amongst locals. Today it's no longer a secret, pulling a steady stream of travellers off the Bruce Highway, halfway between Townsville and Cairns. It's one in a string of watery havens you'll discover nestled in the pine forests behind Cardwell.

Follow the Forest Drive 2.3km out of town and tackle the short trail that leads to Cardwell Lookout and its trio of island vistas (1.6km return walk). Afterwards, drive deeper in the forest to where Attie Creek plunges 30 metres, filling another stunning blue pool before gently cascading over a lip of steep, sheer rock into the eucalypt-forested valley below. The swimming here is divinely chilly and croc-free.

Next up is Dead Horse Creek, which, despite its unfortunate name, is actually a top place to cool off. Soak in the main pool then dare yourself to the waterfall's edge to watch the creek squeeze through a narrow crevice of rock and plunge spectacularly away into a deep, dark, faraway pool. If there's a crowd about, sneak away upstream and rockhop your way to the secluded cascades and secret swimming holes above.

When these pristine waterholes stop flowing at the end of each winter dry season, you can count on Five-Mile Hole to stay deep and full, reviving weary travellers just 8km south of Cardwell. It's a big, beautiful spot to swim with picnic shelters, toilets and gas barbecues provided, signposted just off the Bruce Highway.

🛈 DRIVE THE CIRCUIT

Cardwell is located by the sea, roughly halfway between Cairns and Townsville. To find your way onto the Forest Drive, turn west at the BP fuel station in the centre of town and follow the circuit back to town (26km return). The Spa Pool is at its best just after the wet season (from April) and usually lingers until August.

📍 THE EXPLORER'S PARK

Just 4km north of Cardwell you can walk to the mouth of Wreck Creek in my favourite explorer's own coastal sanctuary – Edmund Kennedy, Girramay National Park (2.5km, 1.5hrs return). Protecting the kind of pristine mangrove streams, tea tree swamps and tangled melaleuca woodlands that thwarted Kennedy on his ill-fated journey to the tip of Cape York in 1848, Edmund Kennedy National Park is a prolific breeding ground for the great flocks of waterbirds you'll undoubtedly spot

🛈 DON'T MISS

Join the Alien Invasion party at Cardwell's own UFO Festival (August) with parades, music, markets and not surprisingly, some serious UFO forums (**cardwellufofestival.com.au**).

HINCHINBROOK ISLAND

Remote and secluded, this is Australia's largest island national park.

Hinchinbrook reclines like a sleeping dragon: a mist-covered, mangrove-fringed spine of rugged, jagged peaks. Sandwiched between the Great Barrier Reef and the ancient forests of the Cardwell Range, Hinchinbrook harbours some of the last wild lands of the tropical far north.

This pristine wilderness seduces adventurers who shoulder packs and escape their realities for four days of hiking on the rugged Thorsborne Trail. Others like me arrive under sail and by sea kayak, to climb to Zoe Bay's skin-tingling waterfall and spot dugongs and sea turtles grazing offshore.

DISCOVER THE HAVEN

Take a boat or paddle your sea kayak to this historical camping spot at Scraggy Point where a stone Indigenous fish trap is clearly visible at low tide. In 1929, island castaways paid one English pound per week to holiday at a guesthouse at The Haven, but they did have to bring their own food.

CASSOWARY COAST
Hinchinbrook Island

WHO WERE THE THORSBORNES?

Arthur and Margaret Thorsborne were local Cardwell conservationists, naturalists and environmental activists whose efforts led to the protection of the Brook Islands, a breeding site for pied imperial-pigeons, located northeast of Hinchinbrook Island. The Thorsbornes' monitoring and lobbying efforts raised the once dwindling population of pigeons on the Brook Islands from 3000 to 40,000, but they didn't stop there. Margaret Thorsborne outlived her husband (who died in 1991) and became an artist and activist for endangered southern cassowaries, mahogany gliders and dugongs. She was awarded an Order of Australia in 2011 for her outstanding conservation efforts, and when she died in 2018, her rainforest sanctuary overlooking Hinchinbrook Island was handed over to Queensland's national park service.

CASSOWARY COAST
Hinchinbrook Island

When I lived in Cardwell I'd wake up to Hinchinbrook Island every morning, and it was the allure of this island that turned me into a sea kayaker and sailor. I launched my first, tiny yacht from a boat ramp in Cardwell, and sailed straight across Missionary Bay to throw down the anchor at beautiful Macushla Beach where a tranquil campground faces the setting sun.

The seagrass beds inside Hinchinbrook Channel nurture great herds of dugongs, and there are no footprints on the island's immaculate, white sand beaches, bordered by the purest of sapphire-hued streams.

PLAN YOUR ESCAPE

Hinchinbrook Island Cruises and Absolute North Charters transfer hikers, campers and castaways from Cardwell and Lucinda to both ends of the Thorsborne Trail (32km, 4 days), and run leisurely, half-day cruises to Ramsay Bay. Download maps and book campsites at parks.des.qld.gov.au.

CASSOWARY COAST
Abergowrie State Forest

ABERGOWRIE STATE FOREST

Explore the forest where Lumholtz found his tree-kangaroos.

At the foot of the Cardwell Range where tree roos and cassowaries roam, Broadwater Creek smooths the river stones, swirling into deep, clear pools and nurturing a creekside sanctuary for Bruce Highway escapees.

On its banks, dominating a rare patch of riparian rainforest, the majestic 200-year-old Broadwater fig arcs across the canopy, luring wompoo pigeons, fairy-wrens and spotted catbirds at dawn. There's a campground with shade aplenty, lovely sandy swimming holes, and upstream, shaded by fan palms, a walking trail hugs the creek to the Overflow.

At this irresistible, summer's day swimming pool, huge granite boulders still the creek, channelling it into chilly spa pools that make for great wildlife watching, 1.5km from the campground. Set out at dawn to spot southern cassowaries and rare Lumholtz's tree kangaroos, which zoologist Carl Lumholtz himself identified in this area back in 1882. After dark, feathertail gliders emerge from their daytime roosts and fireflies appear to guide your nocturnal, torch-lit wandering.

TAKE A HIKE

DALRYMPLE TRACK
Follow this famous former stock route through fan palm forests over the rugged Cardwell Range, crossing a rare, red brick bridge that's been declared a National Trust treasure (4hrs one way).

TAKE A BREAK

Abergowrie State Forest is located 82km southwest of Cardwell. The campground at Broadwater provides wheelchair-accessible toilets, coldwater showers, barbecues, picnic tables, firepits and a swimming pontoon (no pets, BYO firewood). Visit year-round and book campsites online with QLD National Parks.

ATHERTON TABLELANDS

Up the range, an hour's drive west of Cairns, this high-altitude haven harbours cool Mabo forests and volcanic craters, giant fig trees and deep water-filled maars, and dwelling within, some of the tropical north's rarest creatures. Hike in search of Lumholtz's tree-kangaroos on the forested flanks of Mount Hypipamee, photograph Mareeba's own rare rock wallaby at sunset at Granite Gorge, and paddle Lake Tinaroo at dawn to spot platypus as they emerge to feed.

Stretching from Wooroonooran National Park on its southeast fringe to Mareeba in the north, the Atherton Tablelands is dotted with scenic little villages nestled amongst the volcanic hills. All are immensely likeable, but no two are alike. If you can time your trip, you might catch Mareeba's rockingly good rodeo (in July) or Yungaburra's uber cool folk festival (October). Year round you can climb into the canopy on the Mamu Tropical Skywalk and float away from Mareeba, the best place in Australia to go hot air ballooning.

Zillie Falls – page 142.

ATHERTON TABLELANDS
Hot air ballooning

HOT AIR BALLOONING
Slow down, get high and take in the big picture.

Mareeba is the best place in Australia to get carried away. It has the most stable air conditions in the country, and there are over 300 days of sunshine each year. To catch the sunrise and bag some dreamy, misty-morning balloon shots, you're going to have to brave a crack-of-dawn start.

But once you climb into the basket and rise above the world, this wake-up with serious wow-factor will blow you away.

Ballooning is best over the dry, clear winter months. Then, low-lying clouds, low humidity and just a touch of fog on the hilltops create simply stunning big-picture vistas.

📍 GET SKY HIGH

Ballooning is suitable for everyone over four years and winter is the best time to fly. Trips take 30 or 60 minutes and include transfers from Cairns and the northern beaches, breakfast and the obligatory glass of bubbles too (cairnshotairballoon.com.au).

ATHERTON TABLELANDS
Mareeba Rodeo

DON'T MISS
Catch a flick at the Mareeba Drive-in on the Kennedy Highway (its weekend movie sessions are a steal).

MAREEBA RODEO
For the best bull wrangling in the north.

It's a charming country town that foodies adore. But Mareeba flaunts its wild side every July when cowboys and girls arrive to wrangle bulls and broncos in the annual Mareeba Rodeo. Two weeks of events take over the town – horse sports, a ute muster, a downtown parade and rodeo ball – all of which warms up the crowds for one almighty day of wrestling, wrangling and riding.

The action takes place at custom-built Kerribee Park, drawing together a 14,000-strong crowd sporting their best hats and boots, who camp by the rails and make a weekend out of the fun, as they have since 1949.

For the rest of the year, Kerribee Park attracts a quieter crowd: the great mobs of kangaroos that keep the grass down, and the caravanners and campers they entertain at sunset. Kerribee Park is spacious and pet-friendly, with clean facilities and low fees. It's conveniently located 4km from town on the road to Chillagoe.

WILD LIFE
Spend one wild day in Mareeba: climb to the soothing spa pools beneath Emerald Creek Falls (2km return) and picnic downstream. Afterwards, head to Granite Gorge to swim, stroll and watch Mareeba's own endangered rock-wallabies emerge at dusk to play (campsites and cabins available).

ATHERTON TABLELANDS
Granite Gorge rock-wallabies

GRANITE GORGE ROCK-WALLABIES

The granite oasis where rare rock-wallabies play.

In this unexpected labyrinth of balancing boulders and sculpted granite spires, ancient fig trees cast shadows over cool, sandy waterholes and travellers walk and wait for the rock-wallabies that appear at dusk.

When they emerge from their daytime hideouts to feed and laze and bound about on the warm rock slabs, you'll be treated to incredibly close encounters with a species found nowhere else.

Discovered in 1996, the Mareeba rock-wallaby is rare, endangered and utterly enchanting. In Granite Gorge at least, years of hand feeding has made them remarkably stoic to the presence of humans. Encounters take place against a magical backdrop of cliffs, caves and striking rock formations known as Turks Head, Dinosaur Rock and The Arch.

Walking trails elevate you to lofty lookouts over Granite Gorge and lead to the edge of pretty cascades and waterholes (I love the pool beneath Balancing Rocks). Sunset's rosy glow transforms the granite to woo photographers, and during a full moon, the granite is bathed in an ethereal glow. Whether you swim, wildlife watch or wander, allow a couple of end-of-day hours to experience it all.

📍 MAKE IT HAPPEN

Granite Gorge is located 12km from Mareeba. Day visitors, campers and overnight guests are welcome (entry fees apply), and there are toilets and a café on site (**granitegorge.com.au**).

ATHERTON TABLELANDS
Lake Tinaroo

LAKE TINAROO

Paddle with platypus as the mist rises over this World Heritage-listed wonderland.

BYO water toys, select a shady lakeside camp, then get wet any way you can, exploring and playing on the north's most beloved playground. There's barramundi to battle on Tinaroo's shallow, snaggy tributaries, and walking trails to water-filled volcanic craters and giant 500-year-old fig trees.

Uniquely too, Lake Tinaroo is a top spot to encounter platypus. Push off for a silent, pre-dawn paddle just as the early morning mist begins to rise. When conditions are calm, you'll see dozens of tiny platypus duck-diving and floating as they feed.

Paddle away from Lake Tinaroo's open, grassy shores into shallow, protected nooks with overhung banks, or launch your boat from the Tinaburra boat ramp in Yungaburra. Dusk and dawn are the best times to spot platypus, watching for the telltale bubble streams as these tiny monotremes appear.

LOVE TO FISH?

Don't miss the Tinaroo Barra Bash (November).

STAY AND PLAY

Lake Tinaroo is 60km from Cairns via the Gillies Highway. The scenic 28km-long Danbulla Forest Drive circles Lake Tinaroo, leading to five national park campgrounds: School Point, Fong-On Bay, Platypus, Downfall and Kauri Creek. Toilets, picnic tables, water and fire pits are provided, and entry is free (no dogs).

ATHERTON TABLELANDS
Curtain and Cathedral fig trees

THE BIG FIG TREES
Stand in awe of the north's tallest, oldest forest giants.

Just after dawn when the rainforest is barely awake, a shroud of mist rises to reveal the spectacular 500-year-old Curtain Fig Tree, bathed in magical, early morning light. Distinguished by a stunning curtain of hanging aerial roots, this fig tree pierces the canopy near Lake Eacham, towering 50 metres above onlookers who wander, necks craned upwards, along the boardwalk at its base.

Just as old but with grander dimensions and none of the crowds is the nearby Cathedral Fig Tree in Danbulla National Park. It's 12-storeys high and so large you'd need 24 people holding hands just to circle its trunk. Arrive at dawn to enjoy the chorus of birdsong, and return at dusk with a torch to spot long-nosed bandicoots.

📍 TAKE A WALK

Head south of Yungaburra on the Gillies Highway, turn right and follow Curtain Tree Fig Road to the tree (2.5km). The Cathedral Fig Tree is signposted along Danbulla Forest Drive en route to Lake Tinaroo.

ATHERTON TABLELANDS
Mobo Creek Crater

MOBO CREEK CRATER
Unravel the mystery of Mobo Creek.

Deep in the forest where platypus swim, this basalt marr that's both baffling and beautiful rates as my favourite short hike on the shores of Lake Tinaroo. Past fragrant rainforest plants it takes just 15 minutes to reach the bubbling pools on Mobo Creek where you can dangle your feet and stare up into the canopy, and rock hop upstream in search of platypus.

The rainforest is lush and magnificent, but what this walk really showcases is what geologists believed was a water-filled volcanic crater – known as a marr – until they noticed that the old basalt lava appears to flow into, not out of, the crater itself. While others sort out the mystery of this marr, you get to unwind on one of the loveliest walks in the north.

📍 TAKE A HIKE

Mobo Creek Crater is signposted along Danbulla Forest Drive at Lake Tinaroo, 65km from Cairns. The 630m-long circuit walk takes around 15 minutes and is suitable for kids. You can picnic close by at The Chimneys (toilets, barbecues, water and picnic shelters), and take longer bushwalks around Lake Euramoo and Kauri Creek (5km).

ATHERTON TABLELANDS
Lake Eacham

LAKE EACHAM

Chill your bones with a swim inside a volcanic crater.

At 65 metres deep and uber-cold, this water-filled volcanic crater is one of the stranger scuba diving sites in the north. It's calm, clear, and home to saw-shelled turtles that impress kids by breathing through their bottoms. It's also a peaceful place to paddle, swim and SUP, and despite being formed by explosive rising lava, Lake Eacham's setting – surrounded by rainforest and home to musky rat kangaroos and red-legged pademelons – couldn't be more tranquil.

Scuba diving is the most adventurous way to explore, but snorkelling the clear, calm shallows is equally good fun as you search for fish and those impressive saw-shelled turtles. Locals love to picnic on its shores and tackle long training laps across the lake. Bring your own water toys or hire a canoe from nearby Yungaburra Pit Stop en route to the lake. After your chilly dip, you can warm up on the excellent rainforest trail that loops around the water's edge (3km, easy).

⚲ GET WET

Drive south of Cairns to Gordonvale (20km), climb the Gillies Range and take the signposted turn-off to Lake Eacham. There are toilets, picnic tables and a boat ramp by the lake. For scuba adventures, contact **bluedive.com.au**.

ATHERTON TABLELANDS
Yungaburra

YUNGABURRA
Find your new happy place in the north's most colourful village.

Nestled in cool, mabo forests studded with volcanic hills and deep water-filled maars, Yungaburra is a scenic little village, unequalled in the north. It's cute and cool at the same time: one big ole street, an iconic, old-fashioned pub and a string of outdoor cafes, arty gift shops and just a couple of good places to stay.

It's also home to one rockingly laidback folk festival, which takes over the town each October. The Tablelands Folk Festival turns every park, street corner and café into a stage for spontaneous busking sessions, guitar gigs, rowdy bush dances and quirky performance art. The line-up is loud, live and worldly, and the tropical location unique. So, if you time your trip right, you can soak it all up in the shade of a fig tree, sipping slow beers to the sound of didgeridoos and drums.

Yungaburra also happens to be the best place on the Tablelands to spot platypus. Stroll to Petersons Creek at the end of town and sit by the water's edge at dusk or dawn. When you go, don't miss the town's exceptional monthly markets for wholesome food and feel-good shopping.

MAKE IT HAPPEN

Yungaburra is an hour's drive west of Cairns. Arrive in October for the Tablelands Folk Festival (tickets online at tablelandsfolkfestival.org.au). Markets are held on the 4th Saturday of every month from 7.30am-12.30pm (yungaburramarkets.com).

ATHERTON TABLELANDS
Wongabel Forest & Hasties Swamp

WONGABEL FOREST & HASTIES SWAMP
Go where the wild things are.

It's one of Australia's last patches of endangered Mabi forest and so far off the radar that most travellers don't know that Wongabel Forest even exists. That's good news for the Lumholtz's tree-kangaroos that dwell there and the walkers who get to stroll the loop circuit in blissful solitude. Wongabel is a precious remnant of the once expansive Mabi forests that covered the Tablelands 100 years ago.

Today, less than four percent of these forests remain, swamped by a patchwork of agricultural plots and now far too small to support the southern cassowaries and musky rat-kangaroos that have disappeared from much of the Tablelands. It's my favourite place to wander when I need to steal a little solitude, and the easy Heritage Walk takes just an hour, looping 2.5km through the forest.

You don't have to be a twitcher to enjoy time-out with the waterbirds at Hasties Swamp. Indigenous Yidinji people call it Nyleta meaning 'where the waters meet', and these national park-protected wetlands lure vast, colourful flocks of grey teals and pink-eared ducks, egrets, ibis and magpie geese in numbers that swell to 1500.

Stake out the swamp's two-storey bird hide during the dry season when shrinking waters bring birds into close view. Access is free and 24-hour, and there are identification charts for beginner birders, wheelchair (and stroller) access and toilets.

📍 GET YOURSELF WILD

Wongabel Forest is signposted 8km south of Atherton on the Kennedy Highway, 4km past Hasties Swamp on the road to Herberton.

139

MOUNT HYPIPAMEE

Meet Queensland's most captivating kangaroo.

Resembling a cross between a bear and a kangaroo, the far north's most intriguing creature inhabits the canopy of Mount Hypipamee National Park, catching early-morning bushwalkers by surprise. Found in TNQ and nowhere else in the world, Lumholtz's tree-kangaroos - known as Mabi - only occasionally reveal themselves.

Sometimes we get lucky! On one wintry, early morning walk, I was stunned when two tree-kangaroos bounded suddenly across my path. They scampered along the mountainside track before climbing swiftly away into the treetops. With their long tails swinging free, our eyes met in equally curious stares, rendering me spellbound.

Just the thought of glimpsing a tree-kangaroo lures a steady stream of walkers onto Mount Hypipamee's lush volcanic slopes, to follow trails that end at a dramatic crater where sheer granite walls plunge 140 metres. Returning from the crater, walkers linger with cameras poised, cooling their heels in chilly swimming holes beneath the pretty, fern-fringed Dinner Falls.

There may be as few as 2000 Lumholtz's tree-kangaroos left in the wild, so if you don't see one at Mount Hypipamee, head to my secret watching spot at nearby Nerada Tea Plantation, signposted 9km from Malanda. I never believed it would be so easy to see tree-kangaroos here, just outside Nerada's friendly teahouse where you can sip pesticide-free tea and munch on delicious freshly baked scones.

ATHERTON TABLELANDS
Mount Hypipamee

DON'T MISS

Malanda's Tree Roo Awareness Week (May) for feel-good fun and festivities.

TOP TIP

Hit Mount Hypipamee's walking trails early, before the tour buses arrive.

ONE WILD DAY

Mount Hypipamee National Park is located 25km south of Atherton on the Kennedy Highway. There are no entry fees (or camping allowed) but toilets and tables are provided by QLD National Parks. Learn more about Lumholtz's tree-kangaroos and donate at **treeroorescue.org.au**.

ATHERTON TABLELANDS
The Falls Circuit

THE FALLS CIRCUIT

Go chasing waterfalls on the Tablelands' ultimate, wet adventure.

Kick-start a day of watery fun, tripping across the Tablelands to bathe in sunny pools beneath some of the most picturesque, tropical cascades you are ever likely to discover. Clustered around the tiny town of Millaa Millaa and linked by a 16km circuit road, the trio of streams that gather as Zillie, Ellinjaa and Millaa Millaa Falls are popular and easy to access. Further afield, Souita, Pepina and Mungalli Falls are irresistibly secluded, and Malanda Falls offers a top little rainforest hike too.

To get started, join the Falls Circuit 2km south of Millaa Milliaa, travelling anti-clockwise to reach Ellinjaa Falls, signposted 3.5km along Theresa Creek Road.

Ellinjaa Falls

ELLINJAA FALLS

This stunning little waterfall drops 10 metres into a jungle-clad cauldron. It fills a small, circular pool that's shrouded by ferns feeding on the mist and trees that cling impossibly to the sheer walls. To get wet, just stroll down the short trail that winds beneath the falls and dangle your feet as bright dragonflies flit about in the sunshine.

Zillie Falls

ZILLIE FALLS

Reaching Zillie Falls, a 2.4km drive away, is no sweat because this impressive fall is just for looks. From the carpark, a 100m pathway leads to a viewing platform above the falls that overhangs the water shooting over Zillie's sheer rock overhang and the lush, forested valley it fills. Take in the vista then turn back and make a beeline for Millaa Millaa Falls to get yourself wet.

MILLAA MILLAA FALLS

It's renowned as the most perfect of falls, arcing over the edge of a sheer rock amphitheatre in one stunning, glistening veil. At its base, swimmers float in the serene, sandy pool and turtles and eels gather in the shallows. Travellers lounge poolside on grassy lawns, taking dips and Insta shots, and if you linger until the crowds leave, you might spot the platypuses that surface at dusk.

It's here that pioneering explorer Christie Palmerston and his Indigenous guides reportedly set up camp during his 12-day, 100km trail-blazing journey from Geraldton (now Innisfail) to Herberton back in 1882. Today it's a top spot to swim and picnic before finding your way to more secluded falls.

Malanda Falls

ATHERTON TABLELANDS
The Falls Circuit

MUNGALLI FALLS
Drive the Palmerston Highway 13km from Millaa Millaa and follow the signs to Mungalli Falls, which at 90 metres, rates as the highest waterfall on the Atherton Tablelands. The middle tier of the falls is the longest. After you cool your heels with a swim at its base, you can head to Mungalli Creek Dairy for smoothies and samples of biodynamic cheese and yoghurt.

FALLS, GLORIOUS FALLS
If there's time left in your day and you are still in your swimmers, follow the Old Palmerston Highway 10 minutes south of Millaa Millaa to check out Souita and Pepina Falls. Close by, around 20km north of Millaa Millaa, Malanda Falls tumbles over the basalt edge of an ancient lava flow to fill a giant swimming pool just north of the town.

The locals love it, and while the pool at its base is contained by concrete, it's the perfect place to cool down after time exploring on the Rainforest Walk just opposite. At just 1.5km return, this secret wander is easily tackled, but so few people do, you are bound to surprise birds and wildlife.

TAKE THE TOUR

The Waterfalls Circuit begins in Millaa Millaa, located 100km from Cairns on the Atherton Tablelands. Malanda and Millaa Millaa both offer unique B'n'B accommodation or you can camp, swim and spot platypus at Henrietta Creek in Wooroonooran National Park (30km south of Millaa Millaa). Close to Australia's widest flow – Big Millstream Falls – you can free camp at Archer Creek Rest Area (18km from Ravenshoe, toilets provided). Chasing waterfalls is thirsty work, so pack plenty of supplies for a picnic at Millaa Millaa Falls.

Pepina Falls

ATHERTON TABLELANDS
Tablelands Food Trail

TABLELANDS FOOD TRAIL

Got tired tastebuds? Tackle this gastronomic, farm gate adventure.

The far north's new breed of farmers, cheese makers and coffee roasters have opened their gates to tempt travellers with fresh, bio-dynamic dairy products, bush tucker ice-cream, sparkling mango wines and all-day coffee tastings.

Hit the Food Trail at Mungalli Creek's Farmhouse Café outside of Millaa Millaa, to breakfast on fruit yoghurts and bio-dynamic cheeses (and delicious Davison Plum cheesecake), and work your way through the free samples to find your take-home favourites. Close by, Malanda's Gallo Dairyland offers free cheese tastings, milking demonstrations and kids can hand-feed the animals too.

A short drive away in Mareeba, where three quarters of Australia's coffee is grown, local plantations offer excellent farm gate experiences to kick-start your day. Head to Coffee Works for indulgent, all-day sampling of as much coffee, chocolate, tea and liqueur as you like. Jacques Coffee has hour-long coffee tours, tastings and samples, and Skybury is a top spot for lunch and shopping.

Mareeba's distinctly tropical wineries can sell you something surprising to crack at happy hour. For cellar door tastings and sales visit Mt Uncle Distillery at Walkamin, Golden Drop Winery for irresistible sparkling mango wine, and de Brueys for award-winning passionfruit wine and a nip of its Flagship Coffee Elixir made from local beans.

As the day winds down, there are two reasons why you should squeeze in a stop at Nerada Tea. The first is found clinging to the canopy mere metres from the tearoom where travellers relax over pots of freshly brewed tea. Lumholtz's tree kangaroos are rarely seen rainforest dwellers, but the pair that stakes out the trees at Nerada doesn't mind the tea-sipping crowd below and I'm happy to say they have dazzled me too. Nerada offers Devonshire teas and free factory tours too.

ATHERTON TABLELANDS
Mamu Tropical Skywalk

MAMU TROPICAL SKYWALK
Get sky high over the rainforest on this canopy trail.

Climb into the treetops on this great canopy adventure in Wooroonooran National Park. What begins as an easy 2.5km stroll, soon has you daring yourself out onto a cantilever that holds you high above the North Johnstone River gorge far, far below. Next up, wander 350 metres through the rainforest canopy along the Skywalk, ogling birdlife at the very tops of the trees.

The vistas are bewitching, but wait, there's more. Climb the 37 metre-high observation tower for the ultimate bird's-eye view, high above Wooroonooran's misty, rainforest-clad peaks. There's plenty to learn along the way about this forest belonging to Ma:Mu Indigenous people (allow around 90 minutes).

TOP TIP

The operators of Paronella Park (page 116) own the Mamu Tropical Skywalk too, so you'll score a discount if you buy tickets for both attractions online.

GET YOURSELF HIGH

Mamu Tropical Skywalk is located 90 minutes south of Cairns (30 minutes from Innisfail) on the Palmerston Highway. It's open daily from 9.30-5.30pm (mamutropicalskywalk.com.au).

ATHERTON TABLELANDS
Big Millstream Falls

BIG MILLSTREAM FALLS

Save the best 'til last and let Australia's widest falls woo you.

Just off the beaten track but perfect for explorers pushing west across the Savannah, Big Millstream rates as the country's widest, single-drop waterfall, snagged by a broad rock tier that spans Archer Creek.

It's well worth a stop en route to Cobbold Gorge or Undara Lava Tubes to swim in the sunny pool that gathers beneath the falls before ebbing away into the scrub. Self-sufficient campers can overnight downstream at fee-free Archer Creek Rest Area, shaded by towering gums.

SPEND A NIGHT

Follow the Kennedy Highway 18km past Ravenshoe – QLD's highest town – to discover Big Millstream Falls and spend a night on Archer Creek.

ATHERTON TABLELANDS
Wooroonooran National Park

WOOROONOORAN NATIONAL PARK
Discover hidden rainforest waterfalls, far off the beaten track.

Well off the tourist trail and hidden deep within the forests of the Ma:Mu Indigenous people, three stunning waterfalls await bushwalkers. From a base camp at Henrietta Creek campground, you can easily tackle the well-marked trails to Tchupala Falls (1.2km return, 40mins), Wallicher Falls (2km return, easy) and the stunning, 50-metre high Nandroyda Falls (6km return, 2-3hrs).

Grassy and right on the water, Henrietta Creek campground is a spacious spot with lush, forested swimming holes and good facilities in the Palmerston (Doongan) Section of Wooroonooran National Park. Close by you can take in views from Crawfords Lookout and the Mamu Tropical Skywalk.

Nandroyda Falls

◉ WHEN YOU GO

To reach Henrietta Creek Campground, head 25km south of Millaa Millaa on the Palmerston Highway. This large, grassy camp provides picnic tables, free gas barbecues, water and toilets with wheelchair access.

THE WILD WEST

Way out west where the road thins out and brolgas dance on flaxen savannah grasslands, intrepid travellers discover glittering caves and flaring red rock chasms, fossick for aquamarine and agates, and bathe in Innot's scorching hot springs. The big-ticket destinations include Undara's lava tubes and Cobbold Gorge, and if you continue to the far northwest, you can float a boat through Lawn Hill's crimson canyon, carved by the rainbow serpent known as Boodjamulla.

Journey beyond the Atherton Tablelands by train, car or 4WD and find yourself where the big sky vistas begin and agile wallabies graze at sunset. Choose to stick to the bitumen or venture far off track along the excellent, blissfully lonely Burke Developmental Road, which I rate as the best way to get from Chillagoe to Karumba for dreamy sunsets over the Gulf of Carpentaria.

Lawn Hill Gorge – page 168.

THE WILD WEST
Cobbold Gorge

COBBOLD GORGE
Cruise through this faraway chasm in the Savannah's agate country.

Water-rippled walls soar high above, sculpted and aglow in the late afternoon sunlight. Past freshwater crocodiles hauled out on sunny banks, our tiny boat motors deep into the chasm, all eyes lifted skywards at the mesmerising play of light on Cobbold's flaring rock walls.

West from Cairns across the grassy Savannah plains, Cobbold Gorge is a stunning, faraway find with a dozen adventures to tempt travellers off the bitumen. There are cabins and camping, and poolside wining and dining, but it's the gorge itself that will dazzle you most.

My best day at Cobbold Gorge begins with a hike to hidden rock pools upstream on Agate Creek, discovering under crumbling overhangs, treasures that explorer Richard Daintree himself left behind. With appetites sated by home-baked cakes and billy tea, and pockets heavy with bright gemstones gathered on the creek's little-visited upper reaches, I board a boat to cruise quietly through the gorge, legs weary and neck craned upwards.

One of the best things about Cobbold Gorge is that touring options bridge all budgets. There is low-cost camping and free-of-charge kayaking, bushwalking trails, sunset lookouts and an infinity pool for starry-night floating. For around $100 you can join a guided bush tucker walk that climbs high above the gorge to peer into the abyss from Cobbold's magical glass bridge.

My top splurge: fly away to a faraway sunset spot on an end-of-day chopper ride that dips and rolls over rocky scarps for unforgettable views, or simply relax, wine and dine poolside under a big Savannah sky.

WHAT'S SUP?

It's like yoga for water babies and taking a stand up paddleboard through Cobbold Gorge is my all-time favourite way to explore.

MAKE YOUR ESCAPE

Cobbold Gorge is located 85km south of Georgetown, signposted off the Gulf Developmental Road (a six-hour drive west of Cairns). Access to the gorge is by guided tour only: boat rides, walking tours and stand-up paddleboarding. The resort provides campsites, cabins, a restaurant and bar, sells basic supplies, and provides an infinity pool and kayaks free-of-charge (**cobboldgorge.com.au**).

THE WILD WEST
Undara Experience

UNDARA EXPERIENCE
Spotlight your way through Australia's longest lava tubes.

When Undara's volcano erupted, sweeping rivers of molten lava filled every riverbed and watercourse for 160km. It flowed so fast across the Savannah that it could have filled Sydney Harbour in just six days.

190,000 years on, what's left behind are immense, empty tunnels and lava-encrusted caves large enough to walk through. They are so endless that the Ewamian Indigenous people called this place Undara, meaning 'a long way'.

If you've never found yourself inside a lava tube – and one of the world's largest no less – you'll want to make the drive 300km west of Cairns to spotlight underground and witness one of Australia's most incredible natural spectacles.

It all happens on my favourite twilight tour – Wildlife at Sunset – after you sip sparkling wine and the sun dips over an undulating savannah horizon that resembles a Dreamtime caterpillar. When darkness descends on the lava field, you'll be led to the mouth of Barkers Cave to watch the dazzling mass exodus of thousands of tiny insectivorous microbats. As they exit, watch pythons and brown tree snakes battling it out, stretching into the abyss to snare the bats as they fly on by.

Elsewhere at Undara, there are walking trails, antilopine wallaroos to watch, camping and cabins, and big starry nights and storytelling around the campfire. But the best of Undara is found underground, and two tours take you there: the Wind Tunnel Explorer (for thrill-seekers) or the more leisurely Archways Explorer experience.

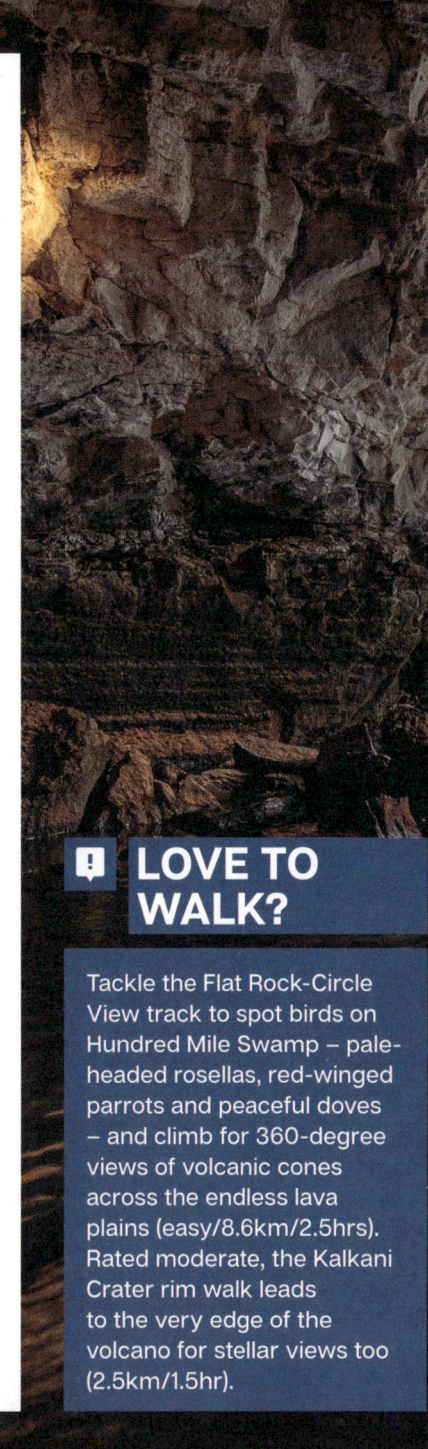

LOVE TO WALK?

Tackle the Flat Rock-Circle View track to spot birds on Hundred Mile Swamp – pale-headed rosellas, red-winged parrots and peaceful doves – and climb for 360-degree views of volcanic cones across the endless lava plains (easy/8.6km/2.5hrs). Rated moderate, the Kalkani Crater rim walk leads to the very edge of the volcano for stellar views too (2.5km/1.5hr).

📍 MAKE IT HAPPEN

Undara Experience (in Undara Volcanic National Park) is a four hour drive southwest of Cairns. Take the signposted turnoff 84km past Mount Garnet and continue for 15km. You'll find campsites, cabins, a swimming pool, restaurant, bar and a range of underground and wildlife tours. Visit over the winter months or arrive in October for Outback Rockabilly Rods & Rides Festival (**undara.com.au**).

THE WILD WEST
Chillagoe Caves

CHILLAGOE CAVES

Descend beneath the scrub into this sparkling underground world.

It's rugged and scrubby and studded with towering limestone, but it's what lies beneath Chillagoe's magnificent karst country that will blow you away. Tunnelled far below town, a labyrinth of caves sparkle with chandeliers and delicate stalactites and shawls, growing and glistening with the rainwater that trickles and splashes into gleaming rimstone pools.

Three caves in Chillagoe are open for business. You can climb, crawl and shimmy through Donna, Royal Arch and Trezkinn Caves on national park ranger-led tours. With a torch and a touch of bravado, you can tackle daring roams on your own into Pompeii and Bauhinia Caves too.

I love Donna Cave for the Cinderella-style Fairy Grotto that shimmers at the bottom of a 200-step staircase, and Royal Arch Cave for its thrilling drop down the sculpted Laundry Chute, feet first. With extraordinary, life-like rock formations (including Queen Victoria at the entrance), a grand tour through Royal Arch Cave leads to the pulpits of Cathedral Chamber, past the famous Limestone Cowboy on horseback and the undeniable profile of the Wicked Witch of Chillagoe.

You're more likely to encounter swiftlets than stalactites in wilder Pompeii and Bauhinia Caves, but descents into these free, self-guided caves are all the more daring because you'll tackle them on your own. Bauhinia is the best (and my eight-year-old can vouch for that), dropping you swiftly and steeply into a pitch-black abyss 10 metres underground where crawl-throughs splinter off into ever-shrinking passageways. Take a torch, a pal and another torch, just in case.

🛈 TIME YOUR TRIP

The Great Wheelbarrow Race takes place each May when charity-minded athletes re-enact the far north's gold rush by pushing wheelbarrows 140km from Mareeba to Chillagoe.

🛈 ROCK YOUR WORLD

Teetering high above Chillagoe, Balancing Rock studs an inspiring scene that's popular for its dramatic sunset silhouettes. The rock is equally stunning and crowd-free at first light and the perfect place for yogis to salute the sun or take time out for quiet meditation before the day-trippers arrive.

📍 GET UNDERGROUND

Chillagoe Caves are 143km west of Mareeba. It's possible to tour Chillagoe in a day, but if you overnight, the Chillagoe Observatory and Eco Lodge have nightly sky shows, cabins and campsites (**coel.com.au**). Book caving tours on arrival at The Hub, open daily from 8am-3.30pm (phone 07 4094 7111).

THE WILD WEST
Ride the Savannahlander

THE SAVANNAHLANDER
Ride the rails west for underground play in caves, lava tubes and Cobbold's incredible outback chasm.

The Sannahlander's shiny silver bullet shoots west, a dashing 1960s-era train that climbs the Kuranda Range high above Cairns and rolls across a rugged landscape tunnelled with volcanic tubes, sandstone chasms and a glittering limestone underworld.

Four-day rail adventures provide easy passage to outback tropical towns and scenes you'd never glimpse from the road, and this is one of the best ways to tick off time at three of the best sights in the west: Chillagoe Caves, Undara Experience and Cobbold Gorge.

You might tackle a shorter rail loop, but you'll struggle to decide which of these three top destinations to give up, and really, all are well worth seeing. Riding the Savannahlander is definitely a trip for lovers of slow travel, allowing you to sit back, take your hands off the wheel and let the gently shifting scenes outside the train woo you.

From rainforested waterfalls to ragged limestone spires, glittering decorated caves and shadowy volcanic tunnels, the sights out west are utterly enchanting and entirely underestimated. You'll spot a surprisingly diverse array of wildlife on leisurely walks, and from your train window too. One unexpected joy of travelling this route by train is the nights you'll get to spend in authentic towns that are far off the tourist track, and all yours to discover.

📍 RIDE THE RAILS

Plan and book your rail time at **savannahlander.com.au**.

159

THE WILD WEST
Mungana Archways

MUNGANA ARCHWAYS
Find fern-filled grottos and deep, dark caves.

It's half-hiking, half-caving, and although it's all above-ground, you'll need a torch to navigate the ever-narrowing chasms tunnelled through Mungana Archways, 20km west of Chillagoe. There's one walking trail and a hundred tiny detours to follow in this maze of collapsed rock that caving buffs call a 'grike field'.

Enter through a gap in the towering limestone bluff, and navigate your way through skinny passageways to discover tiny, fern-filled grottos. Disappear into ever-narrowing chasms, watching the amazing play of midday-light where it enters and illuminates Mungana's collapsed caves.

In its deep and darkest recesses, torch beams will illuminate stalactites and stalagmites working ever so slowly to meet each other. Then there are slender squeezes and crawl-throughs that rarely tempt me onwards! The trail's distance is short – just 160m – but if you've got an adventurous streak and like to climb, or simply want to stop and relish the cool and quiet, allow at least an hour to explore.

Afterwards, find your way to the nearby picnic area and a gallery of Indigenous rock art that adorns the overhung rock wall. Just opposite the rock art, a narrow, unmarked (and sometimes very overgrown) trail shoots through the scrub to Old Mungana Cemetery and a handful of pioneer graves.

📍 GET YOURSELF THERE

Mungana Archways is located 20km west of Chillagoe and is signposted off the Burke Developmental Road. If you are well-stocked and self-sufficient, the rugged, corrugated route west pushes all the way to Karumba on a grand off-road adventure that rates as one of my favourites.

THE WILD WEST
Innot Hot Springs

INNOT HOT SPRINGS
Heavenly hot springs for the utterly fearless.

These hot springs are a real scorcher, bubbling to the surface at between 80 and 90°C and at times, literally boiling the sandy pools along Nettle Creek. With water this red-hot, you'll want to test a toe before taking the plunge. Find a traveller who doesn't look lobster-red and slide on in next door to them.

When you go, keep a tight grip on kids who can easily burn themselves, but when you find the pool that's right for you, simmer for a little while to let the springs' renowned curative properties work their magic.

📍 FEEL THE BURN

Discovered in the 1870s by grazier John Atherton (of Atherton Tablelands fame), Innot Hot Springs is located on private property (hence the entry fee), 44km west of Ravenshoe on the Gulf Developmental Road. There's a campground, a café and fuel for sale too. Stop by en route to Undara and Cobbold Gorge.

O'BRIENS CREEK
Find your fortune on this far west fossicking adventure.

The topaz at O'Briens Creek is so easy to find, even the bowerbirds fill their nests with it. I've seen it, and it's true. Even local expert Simon Harrison jokes that he used to have to hide behind trees to stop the topaz jumping out at him.

These days you're going to have to dig a little deeper, and that's half the fun.

Harrison runs the ultra-friendly O'Briens Creek Campground and hands out licences, free fossicking gear and lots of advice about the best places in the nearby public reserve to dig up big, shiny chunks of aquamarine and topaz.

Nothing turns your day in the dust around quite like discovering something shimmering in your pan. The little crystals we dug up weren't enough to retire on, but every thrilling discovery spurred us on to unearth more and more pieces of topaz until, by day's end, we could hold our own amongst the real gem hunters gathered around the campfire.

O'Briens Creek is an easy-to-access fossicking site with gem-quality blue topaz, aquamarine, citrine and smoky quartz that's all yours to unearth. But it's Harrison's camp that puts this place on the map for its lovely waterfront camps, the mesmerising birdlife that gathers at dusk and dawn, and the roaring nightly campfires where travellers talk topaz long after dark.

THE WILD WEST
O'Briens Creek

🛈 GEMS AND GOLD

If you are heading west and love gems, stop at Georgetown to ogle the massive gemstone collection on show at TerrEstrial. Self-sufficient travellers can free camp 20km west of town at the Cumberland Historic Mine Site.

📍 GET FOSSICKING

Drive 285km west of Cairns to Mount Surprise and continue 35km to O'Briens Creek Campground on the banks of Elizabeth Creek. This pet-friendly camp offers unpowered campsites, free use of fossicking gear, on-the-spot fossicking licences and hot showers too (find them on Facebook).

KARUMBA
Get far, far away for famously good fishing and over-the-sea sunsets.

With its irresistible, end-of-the-road ambience, Karumba really is as much fun as people say. Especially if you have fish dinners and dreamy Gulf of Carpentaria sunsets on your mind. There's barramundi to chase up the Norman River, and blue salmon and mackerel off the waterfront's mangrove-fringed shallows (plus cobia, fingermark and queenies too!).

At day's end, travellers all over town gather together for lively fish barbecues, to share secret spots over sundowners and find out who caught what, where and how. But even if you are not a great angler, Karumba has enormous pulling power.

My idea of a great day in Karumba is spent tracking wild things out of the water. Stroll the boardwalk that leads behind the mouth of the Norman River to where agile wallabies graze amongst the mangroves. Then drive to the roadside lagoons on the outskirts of town to capture stunning sunset silhouettes of brolgas performing their hypnotic mating dances.

The town's only watering hole – The Sunset Tavern – serves up chilled ales

🛈 TOP TIP
If you are camping at Karumba Point Holiday and Tourist Park, the free Saturday night fish barbecues are loads of fun, from May to August (karumbapoint.com.au).

THE WILD WEST
Karumba

from every corner of the country and fresh seafood dinners devoured on its shady, frangipani-scented lawns. Arrive in time to salute another watery sunset, or find quietude by driving the sandy 4WD tracks that parallel the beach north to enjoy your own private twilight.

There's a lot of fun to be had in Karumba, and despite its remote location, the town supplies all the essentials with a couple of laidback places to eat and a bustling weekend market during the winter months. Even though I'm a terrible angler, for me, Karumba's pristine slice of prime, Gulf of Carpentaria seaside is always worth the drive.

PUT YOURSELF IN THE PICTURE

Karumba is located 750km west of Cairns via sealed roads. Visit from May to September for cool, dry days and don't miss the Karumba Barra and Blues Anglers Classic (October) for a share of more than $25,000 in prizes (**carpentaria.qld.gov.au**).

DRIVE CAIRNS TO KARUMBA, THE BACK WAY
Rumble off the bitumen at Chillagoe to tackle this 500km-long off-road adventure, traversing a remote landscape of rugged limestone outcrops, flaxen grasslands and lily-covered lagoons. The shady riverside camps along the Burke Developmental Road offer nothing but solitude, campfire dinners and wildlife encounters, making this an exhilarating escape for well-prepared travellers with plenty of fuel, food and spares on board (dry season access only).
For inspiration and to put yourself in the picture, head to **wildtravelstory.com** and click on the videos to see my own family adventuring underground at Chillagoe and tackling this wild, remote run to Karumba.

THE WILD WEST
Leichhardt Falls

LEICHHARDT FALLS
Camp above QLD's most pristine river.

A day's drive west of Normanton where the Savannah Way turns rugged, the Leichhardt River plunges over the edge of a broad, arcing fall. Over the dry season, when the road becomes passable, you can take in its dramatic flurry of whitewater from a camp high on its riverbanks, parking your off-road rig in the shade of pandanus palms and towering eucalypts.

These rustic bush camps are some of the Savannah Way's best, even though they offer nothing but grand views. Bending the canopy, enormous flocks of sulphur-crested cockatoos herald the dawn, while waterbirds stalk the river's edge in silent fishing sessions.

The deep pools beneath the falls are off limits to swimmers because of crocodiles, but look for Indigenous grinding slits on the exposed river bedrock near the causeway.

Named after explorer Ludwig Leichhardt it is one of the few long, Queensland waterways in near-pristine condition. What's more, rare, prehistoric fossils, including an unidentified marsupial unearthed in 2011, have been found along its 621km-long riverbed.

GET THERE

Leichhardt River is 150km west of Normanton along the Savannah Way. There are no facilities and no time limits on your stay

GREGORY RIVER
Headed to Lawn Hill Gorge? This is where free campers find nirvana along the way.

The stranger figs and towering Livistona rigida palms that fringe the Gregory River's translucent flow, shade wintertime travellers too. From camps on its pebbly banks, they plonk their chairs in the shallows and chat, paddle kayaks far upstream, and wander into town for cool, sunset beers and ice creams at the historic Gregory Downs Hotel.

It's the only business keeping this tiny town from turning ghostly but that doesn't deter self-sufficient campers. Gregory's shady camp is free, and although it has a habit of hijacking the best-laid travel plans, you won't find a prettier bush camp anywhere from Karumba to Lawn Hill Gorge.

What I love about this one-more-day destination is the rope swing that dangles midstream and the swift current that sends you shooting downstream on your back to trot back along the pebbly banks for ride after ride. Paddle your kayak far upstream to where the rapids turn you around again, and spot wallabies that drink at the water's edge, waterbirds and kingfishers, and the cockatoos that screech from the paperbarks.

JOIN THE FUN

The 43km-long Gregory River Canoe Marathon is one of Australia's most isolated canoe races, transforming Gregory every May long weekend (**northwestcanoeclub.org.au**).

GET YOURSELF THERE

Drive 420km south of Karumba on the Wills Developmental Road. Gregory has a hotel, playground, toilets, cold water showers and drinking water but no mobile reception. There's a campground by the bridge (with toilets) and bush camping by the river (**burke.qld.gov.au**).

THE WILD WEST
Lawn Hill Gorge

LAWN HILL GORGE

Paddle, hike and snorkel this phenomenal outback oasis.

Waanyi elders say that the rainbow serpent – the Boodjamulla – carved Lawn Hill's emerald, palm-fringed waterway deep into the sandstone plateau, greening an oasis for freshwater crocodiles and flying foxes, wallaroos and fairy-wrens.

Wooing the paddlers who come to glide beneath its soaring crimson cliffs, this remote canyon in Queensland's rugged northwest is one my favourites for its excellent riverside camps and all the ways you get to explore. Challenging trails elevate hikers to gorge-side lookouts, but the most fun to be had at Boodjamulla National Park happens with a paddle in your hands.

Push off from your riverside campsite on this 6km-long canoe adventure beneath blazing red rock that shoots skyward. Upstream through a vivid maze of fan palms and water lilies, Indarri Falls snags Lawn Hill Creek sending it cascading over a broad, two-metre-high drop into deep, crystal-clear swimming holes.

🛈 TOP TIPS

Bring your own kayak, canoe or SUP to explore the gorge at any hour (long before the canoe rental desk opens). With just 20 spacious sites available in Boodjamulla's national park camp, you'll need to book yours well in advance for peak wintertime stays

THE WILD WEST
Lawn Hill Gorge

Tie your boat up here and leap overboard to snorkel with fat barramundi and snapping turtles, and to pummel your muscles beneath Indarri's invigorating, miniature falls. For solitude and the chance to play with the tiny, spitting archerfish that leap clean out of the water to nibble your finger, portage your boat around Indarri Falls and paddle all the way to the racy cascades at the end of Upper Gorge. This is a top spot to go ashore for a picnic too.

Of Boodjamulla's excellent hiking trails, Wild Dog Dreaming is my favourite for its Waanyi rock art and the wild lookout at trail's end where freshwater crocodiles bask on sunny riverbanks and little red flying-foxes bend the canopy above (4.5km/1.5hrs return). Climb the Constance Range for sunset, and you'll be blown you away by what you see. Pack a head torch (and a drone) and set out around 4pm (3 hours return).

PLAN YOUR ESCAPE

Boodjamulla National Park is located in Queensland's far northwest corner, 100km west of Gregory Downs via the Wills Developmental Road (free entry). I like Boodjamulla's affordable national park campsites for their easy access to the water, with coldwater showers, drinking water, tables and toilets supplied. If you crave hot showers, stay at Adels Grove, outside the national park (adelsgrove.com.au). Visit from May to September.

THE WILD WEST
Hells Gate

HELLS GATE
End your TNQ savannah adventure on a high.

For travellers heading west, Hells Gate is where you get to farewell Queensland, standing atop great bulging sandstone buttresses and the crumbling canyons that interrupt the endless savannah plains below.

Reminisce and reflect as you stoke your last starry night Queensland campfire, then rise at dawn and set your sights west to tackle the steep climb up onto the Northern Territory's Barkly Tablelands where roads crumble into corrugations and dip to translucent, pandanus-fringed rivers.

A traditional resting spot for all kinds of travellers, Hells Gate is one of my favourite Savannah Way campsites. Its wild and rocky lookouts are scorching under the midday sun but turn utterly enchanting when the light softens at sunset.

📍 TOP UP YOUR TANKS

For early Australian settlers, Hells Gate was as far as police escorts would accompany them, before abandoning them to brave the NT's high country all alone. Today, it's the last place to get fuel and powered campsites on the 300km stretch across the NT border to Borroloola. The best travel is from June to August. (**hellsgateroadhouse.com.au**)

TRAVEL IN TROPICAL NORTH QUEENSLAND

In the wild, World Heritage-listed, Tropical North Queensland you can travel any way you want, but be warned: the adventures out of Cairns are bigger and bolder than elsewhere in Oz.

In the far tropical north, you don't just go for a swim, you boat to a barely-there sand cay and snorkel with green sea turtles and reef sharks. And when Cairns locals go fishing, they chase coral trout out on the reef and compete with upriver crocs for their share of the big barra.

From Cairns to the tip of Cape York, the beaches are lonely and endless and hugged by coconut palms, and you can spend all day only in a pair of shorts or swimmers. If you're craving time-out with a tropical twist, here are my top tips for getting yourself to Queensland's north.

Sunset on western Cape York.

GETTING TO TROPICAL NORTH QUEENSLAND

By Air
Direct flights to Cairns depart from most Australian capital cities (from Perth and Hobart you may need to touch down in Melbourne or Sydney en route). Before you fly, jump online to book an airport shuttle for travel into the Cairns CBD.

Keen to get beached?
Head straight from the airport to Port Douglas for instant beach time and easy access to the rainforests of Daintree National Park. Shuttle buses depart right outside the airport, but it's best to book in advance.

By Road
The Bruce Highway stretches 1680km along Queensland's east coast from Brisbane to Cairns, leapfrogging between stellar destinations all the way north. From the west, you can follow the adventurous, off-road Savannah Way across the top of Australia from Broome, or stick to sealed routes that push north from Mt Isa.

From Cairns, the very scenic Captain Cook Highway hugs the Coral Sea coastline to Port Douglas, and driving north across the Daintree River, you can follow Cape Tribulation Road and the 4WD-only Bloomfield Track all the way to Cooktown.

To continue further north, you'll need a 4WD and the abilty to camp self-sufficiently in very remote wilderness.

TRAVEL IN TROPICAL NORTH QUEENSLAND

WHEN TO VISIT

The Dry Season

Clear skies, mild temperatures and most importantly – stinger-free seas – all make the dry season, from May to October, the best time to explore the tropics. I like travelling in the crowd-free shoulder months – May or September – when rain rarely interrupts your adventures, and campgrounds, hotels, tracks, trails and tours are never full. Prices at this time can be just a little cheaper, and service is all the more personable when hotels and tour operators have fewer guests to please.

The Wet Season

From November to April, summer in Tropical North Queensland can get hot and humid, but rain rarely lasts for long and usually won't interrupt on-road touring or your reef adventures (just don a stinger-proof suit and get wet).

Over the wet season, waterfalls are at their most spectacular, but you'll need to exercise caution when swimming. Immediately after big downfalls, popular waterholes can become muddied and inundated with debris such as fallen logs, making them hazardous for swimming. Just about every year in the north, someone falls or dives into a waterhole to their death. Never swim in waterholes in flood and always slide, never dive, into them.

WHERE TO STAY

Camping

While this book isn't specifically about camping, the nature of far north Queensland lends itself to travellers who don't mind roughing it a little.

The vast majority of campsites mentioned within are managed by Queensland National Parks. And in nearly every case, they cost just $6.65 per person, per night, or $26.60 for a family (which is one or two adults and up to six children), or are free. It's very good value. Most must be booked online, in advance (at least before you run out of mobile phone coverage) by visiting **parks.des.qld.gov.au**. WikiCamps is a popular app to find campsites in QLD.

Something more solid

Even if you don't travel with your home, TNQ has no shortage of accomodation options, even in the remote reaches of Cape York. Around Cairns, Atherton and the Cassowary Coast, you can stay in anything, from inexpensive hostels to 5-star resorts, although the cabin and bungalow accomodation at caravan parks is often the best value and very family friendly.

As you travel into the more remote areas, many of the roadhouses, old telegraph stations and pubs have cottoned onto the rise in tourism, and so provide good, and often distinct options for travellers. The old first-class train carriages at Undara Experience (page 155) are a recommended stand-out.

WHAT TO PACK

Dress for the heat in lightweight, breathable clothing made from natural (preferably organic) fibres. Pack hats, reef-friendly sunscreen, natural insect repellent, stinger-proof suits or wet suits (for wet season visits), adventure sandals instead of hiking boots, refillable water bottles, quick-dry towels and a sense of adventure.

TRAVEL IN TROPICAL NORTH QUEENSLAND

DRIVING DRAMAS
Off-road Adventures

The bitumen only takes you so far in the north, so if you've got a hankering to get lonely for a while, you're going to need a sturdy, high-clearance 4WD vehicle, with recovery gear, camping equipment and a self-sufficient mindset.

Whether you bring your own or hire one upon arrival in Cairns, if off-roading the north sounds like your kind of fun, keep these tips in mind when you rumble off the bitumen.

Check the tides before taking your 4WD onto the beach and if you get bogged or break down in a remote region and can't get moving again, stay with your vehicle. It will provide shelter and shade, and make you easier to locate from the air. More people die from exposure walking to get help than staying with their vehicle.

Your survival may depend on whether you packed adequate supplies (water, food, a first aid kit, fuel, recovery gear, tools and basic car parts), and if you told someone

AVOIDING ROAD KILL
The further west you travel from Cairns, the more likely you are to encounter wandering cattle, wild pigs and a cavalcade of natives that includes kangaroos, wallabies, and in Mission Beach and the Daintree, southern cassowaries too.
Cattle often graze on the roadside at night, and at dawn and dusk, native animals (especially agile wallabies) can appear out of nowhere. Any animal collision is an utterly disturbing incident that will usually leave you with a dead creature, a dented bull bar or shattered windscreen, and a lump in your throat.
Avoid driving at night, reduce your speed at dawn and dusk, and keep an eye on the road verge at all times.

177

where you were headed and when you were due back.

Most off-road incidents (such as collisions or roll-overs) can be avoided simply by slowing down on unsealed roads. Watch out for road trains and always give them right-of-way on narrow roads.

If you are not travelling on bitumen surfaces, let your tyres down a little – it will improve the ride and comfort, and prevent you from getting punctures as easily. Just remember to slow down a little, too. If the ground is really soft, like on sand, consider letting your tyres down to 15psi. Just remember to pump them back up again when you're back on the blacktop.

Wet Season Floods:
Severe flooding events are rare around Cairns, but they can strand travellers on uninhabited stretches of road, and swell river crossings making them dangerous to attempt.

During the wet, never try to cross flooded bridges or causeways. If crocodiles are around or if the crossing is too deep, find another route or simply wait – most flash floods recede within 24 hours.

BE CROC-AWARE

I find crocodiles utterly fascinating, but since getting close to them is often hazardous to your life, you're going to need to know where you can and can't swim.

The biggest myth about the world's largest reptile is that saltwater (or estuarine) crocodiles live only in saltwater. Actually, salties can make their way into waterholes, creeks and rivers far inland, and are regularly spotted on islands and sand cays across the Great Barrier Reef.

From the 1940s to 1960s, crocodiles were hunted to the brink of extinction in Australia for their skins and for sport. But by 1974, both fresh and saltwater crocodiles had become protected by law. Today, these superior hunters dominate the far north's food chain. They can reach speeds of around 10km/h in short bursts, stay underwater for at least an hour by slowing their heart rate, and are the most proficient hunters in the country.

THINGS THAT STING

Every year from October to May, Irukandji and box jellyfish inhabit Australia's northern beaches. If encountered, they inflict excruciating, potentially fatal stings that require immediate medical attention.

These marine stingers breed up rivers and migrate downstream with wet season downpours to drift along the coast. They are more numerous after rain, and when seas are warm and calm, and although attacks occur every year, the best way to stay safe is to slip on a Lyrca stinger suit before you get wet.

Swimming inside stinger-resistant beach enclosures (at Palm Cove, Ellis Beach and Four Mile Beach for example) can protect against box jellyfish stings, but tiny Irukandji

5 CROC-SAFE RULES

1. Swim with care: always obey signage and if in doubt, stay out of the water.
2. When boating or fishing in rivers, estuaries, tidal areas or deep, murky pools, keep your arms and legs inside the boat.
3. On Cape York, camp well back from the water's edge, avoid repetitive behaviour and don't lure salties by preparing food, gutting fish or washing dishes right by the water.
4. Take care at night when estuarine crocs are more active. With excellent night vision and the ability to remain underwater for up to an hour, crocs may be lurking even when you can't see them. Try shining your torch across the water after dark to spot all those red eyes gleaming back at you.
5. Be extra careful on the water from September to March when crocodiles breed and can become extremely aggressive.

jellyfish can swim straight through the nets.

The only way to prevent contact (other than by sticking to inland waterholes) is to wear a full-body stinger suit (or wetsuit) when swimming, snorkelling, beach fishing and kayaking in the ocean. They may not be particularly flattering, but they can save your life.

If you get stung, dose the affected area liberally with vinegar (do not rub) and seek immediate medical help.

WARD OFF MOSQUITOES

Here's the world's cheapest mossie hack: take a shower. You read right, and the reason it works is because mosquitoes are expert detectors of body odour – caused by the bacteria that cultivate on our skin when we sweat and don't wash it off – and lactic acid, which we expel through our skin through sweat. When you wash without using perfumed soap or spraying fragrant antiperspirants, mosquitoes are much less attracted to you!

If showers are scarce, a tea-tree based repellent is the best bet, for you and the environment.

HIKING IN THE TROPICS

The Wet Tropics rainforests are full of challenging trails that get you far off the beaten track and into the wild. So far in fact, that you'll need to be completely self-sufficient and carry an emergency communicator (an PLB, Garmin Inreach or similar device) to alert emergency services if something goes wrong or you lose your way.

Always carry a head torch, a water treatment system (such as a Steripen), and a first aid kit that can treat snakebites, fractures and dehydration, and know how to use it. Be aware that in the closed canopy of the rainforest, daylight disappears much earlier in the day, so allow plenty of time to finish your walk or get to your chosen campsite before you lose light.

TRAVEL IN TROPICAL NORTH QUEENSLAND

EATING LOCAL

There are some incredible restaurants, eateries and cafes scattered across TNQ, and some in the most unexpected places (like the restaurant at Punsand Bay, 30-minutes from the most northerly tip of mainland Australia). But to really eat local, learn about the foods Indigenous Australia relied on for thousands of years. The north is abundant in bush tucker, and there's no better authority than Les Hiddins. Subscribe to **bushtuckerman.com.au**, to get the best info on what native foods are near where you're travelling.

NEED HELP IN AN EMERGENCY?

Phone 000 for police, ambulance or fire assistance, regardless of where you are in the tropics: on a bushwalking trail, remote 4WD track, or offshore island.

EMERGENCY+ APP
This free-to-download, Australian government-funded app can help pinpoint where you are and mobilise emergency services to get to you as quickly as possible. It's called Emergency+ App, and it uses the GPS functionality of your smartphone to establish your precise location in the event of an accident. All you do is click on the app, hit 'call 000', read your GPS coordinates off the phone screen, and help will be on its way (find out more at **emergencyapp.triplezero.gov.au**).

RESPECT THE REEF: CORAL-SAFE SUNSCREEN

You've travelled a long way to experience the wonders of the Great Barrier Reef, so be sure you don't trash it with toxic sunscreen when you swim. You may not realise it, but most sunscreens sold in Australia (and elsewhere around the world) contain ingredients that have been proven to damage and/or bleach coral reefs.

HOW TO YOU KNOW WHAT TO BUY?
Avoid all sunscreens containing: oxybenzone (also known as benzophenone-3) and octinoxate – both are linked to coral bleaching and have been banned in Hawaii from 2021. For a coral-safe, human-friendly sunscreen, look for one that uses titanium dioxide to shield your skin from harmful solar rays, and contains no nanoparticles which are known to cause developmental disorders in sea life. Old-fashioned zinc oxide is fine, but avoid any 'clear zincs' that contain ingredients highly toxic to sea life.

MAPS OF TROPICAL NORTH QUEENSLAND

This is a big place, and there's a lot to see. Use these maps as you plan your trip and work out which order you should explore the far north of QLD.

Cape Melville, Cape York

MAPS
Great Barrier Reef

MAPS
Port Douglas and Daintree

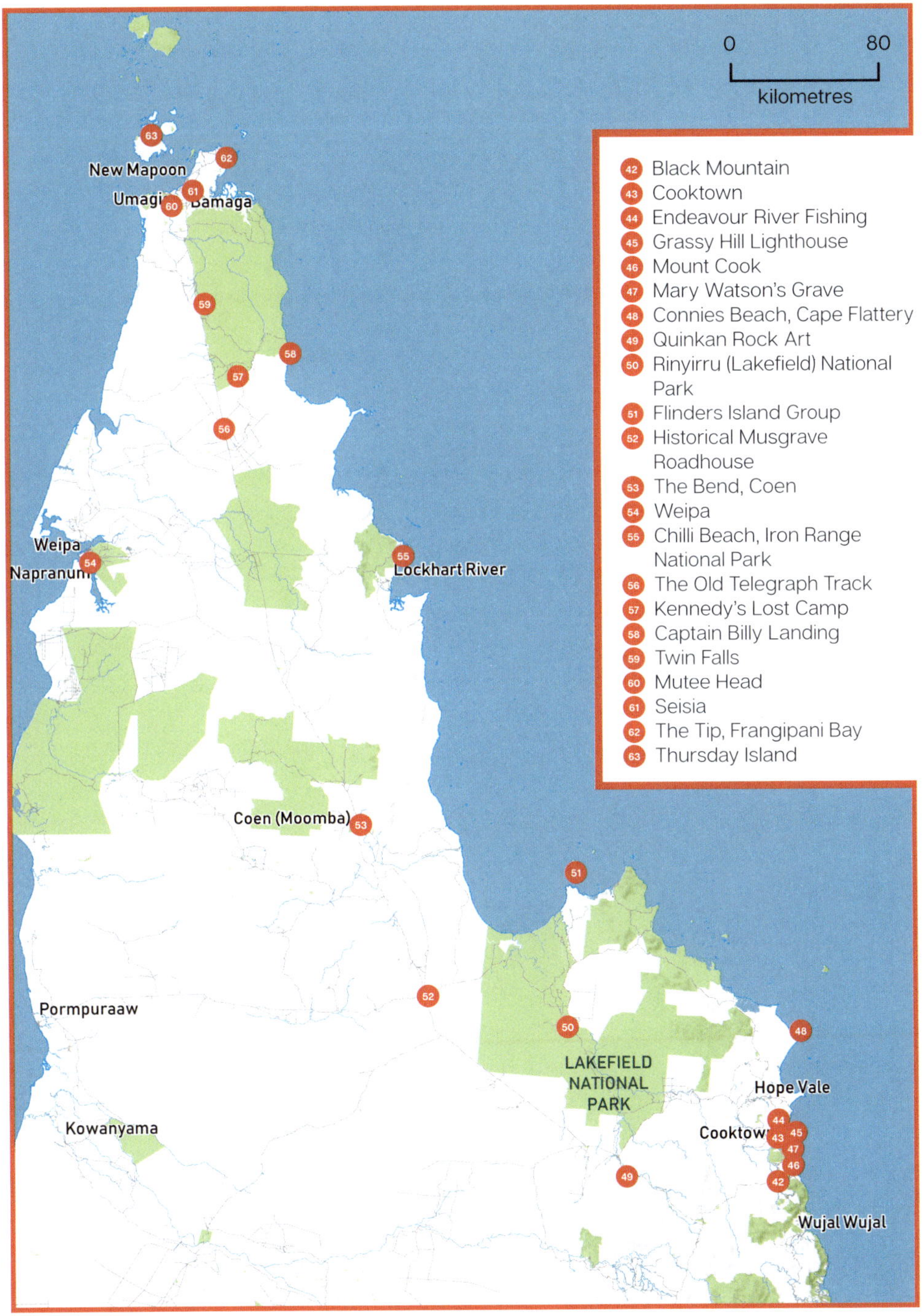
0
80
kilometres
42 Black Mountain
43 Cooktown
44 Endeavour River Fishing
45 Grassy Hill Lighthouse
46 Mount Cook
47 Mary Watson's Grave
48 Connies Beach, Cape Flattery
49 Quinkan Rock Art
50 Rinyirru (Lakefield) National Park
51 Flinders Island Group
52 Historical Musgrave Roadhouse
53 The Bend, Coen
54 Weipa
55 Chilli Beach, Iron Range National Park
56 The Old Telegraph Track
57 Kennedy's Lost Camp
58 Captain Billy Landing
59 Twin Falls
60 Mutee Head
61 Seisia
62 The Tip, Frangipani Bay
63 Thursday Island
New Mapoon
Umagi
Bamaga
Weipa
Napranu
Lockhart River
Coen (Moomba)
Pormpuraaw
Kowanyama
LAKEFIELD NATIONAL PARK
Hope Vale
Cooktow
Wujal Wujal

MAPS
Cassowary Coast

MAPS
Atherton Tablelands

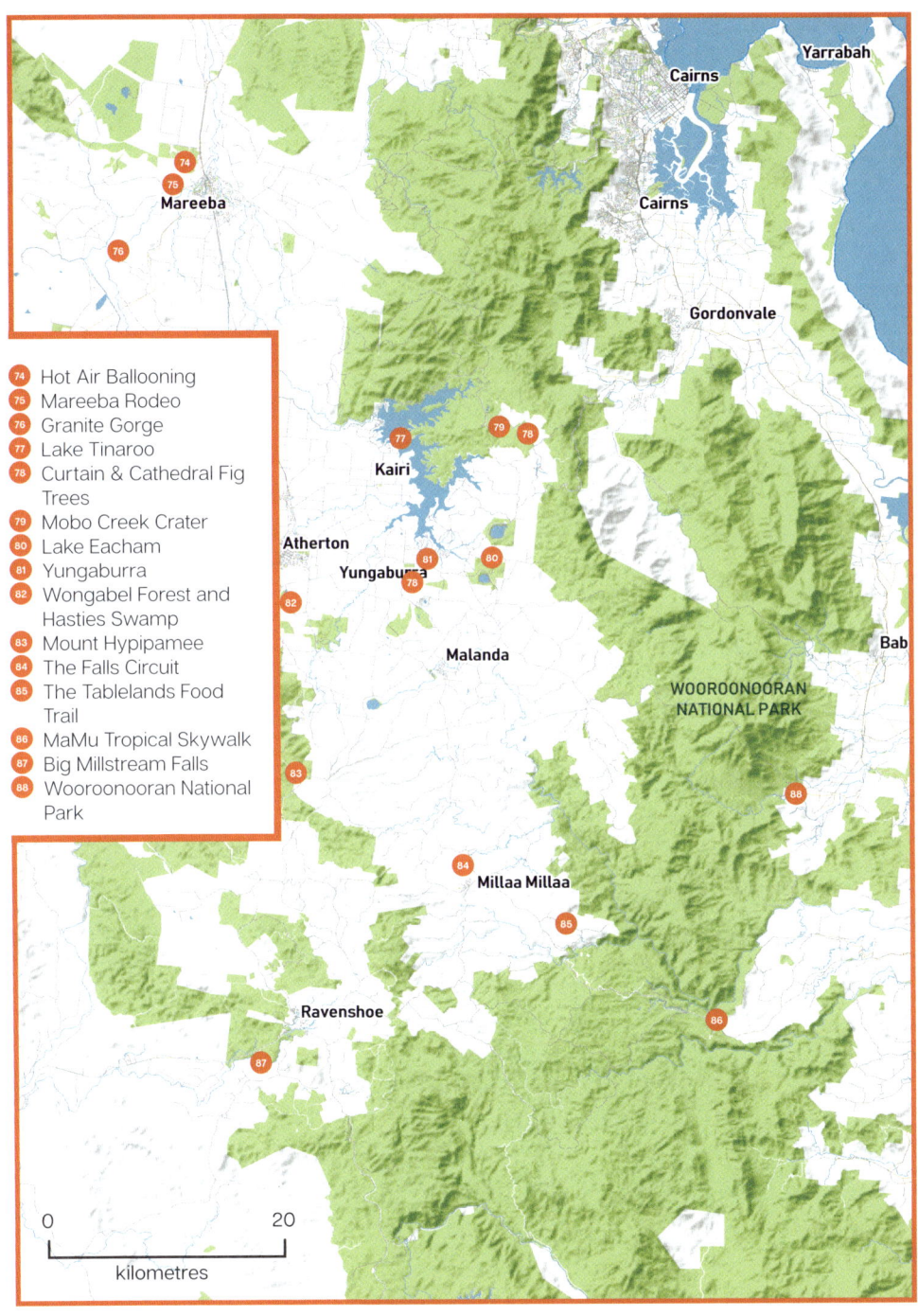

- 74 Hot Air Ballooning
- 75 Mareeba Rodeo
- 76 Granite Gorge
- 77 Lake Tinaroo
- 78 Curtain & Cathedral Fig Trees
- 79 Mobo Creek Crater
- 80 Lake Eacham
- 81 Yungaburra
- 82 Wongabel Forest and Hasties Swamp
- 83 Mount Hypipamee
- 84 The Falls Circuit
- 85 The Tablelands Food Trail
- 86 MaMu Tropical Skywalk
- 87 Big Millstream Falls
- 88 Wooroonooran National Park

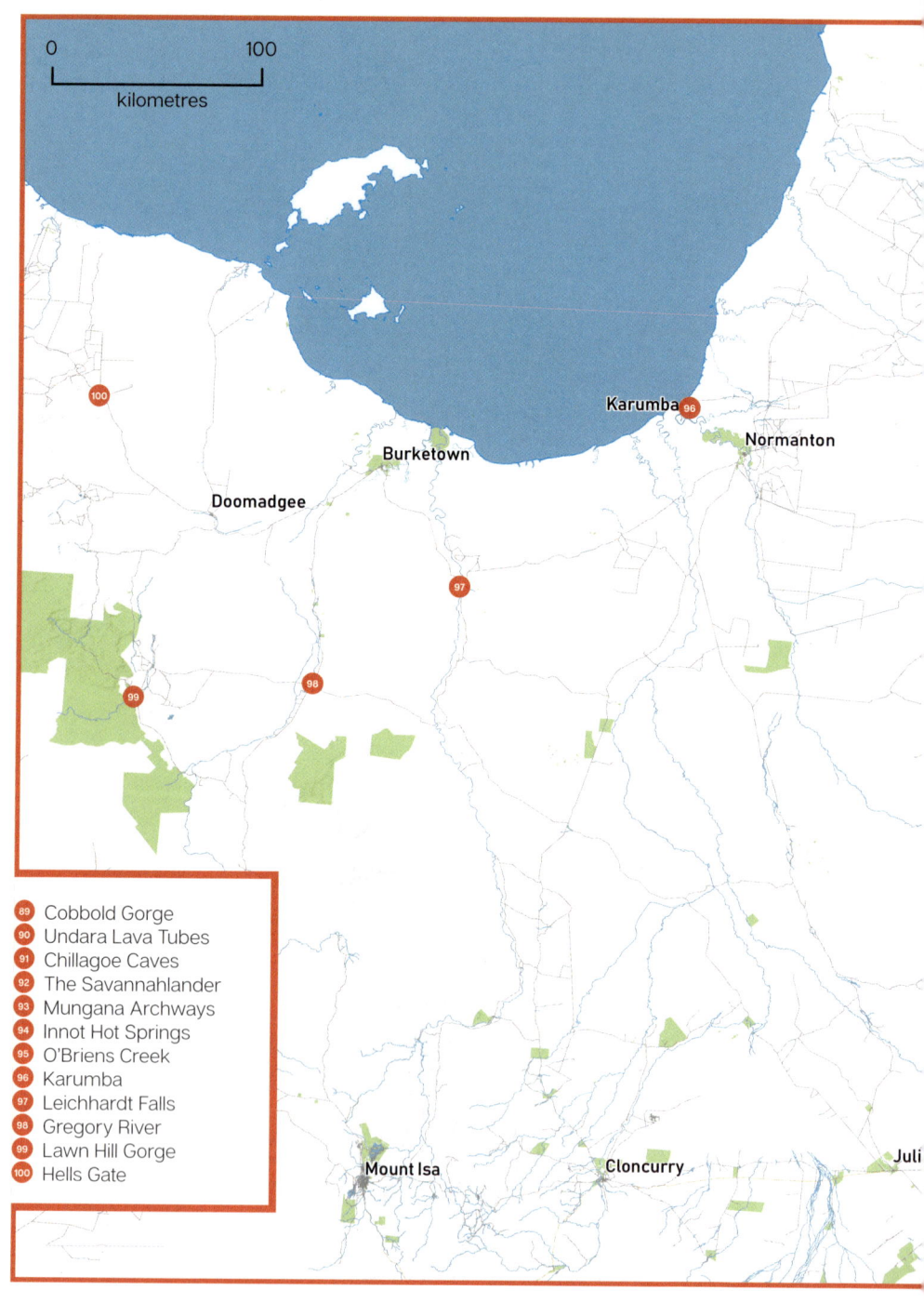

MAPS
The Wild West

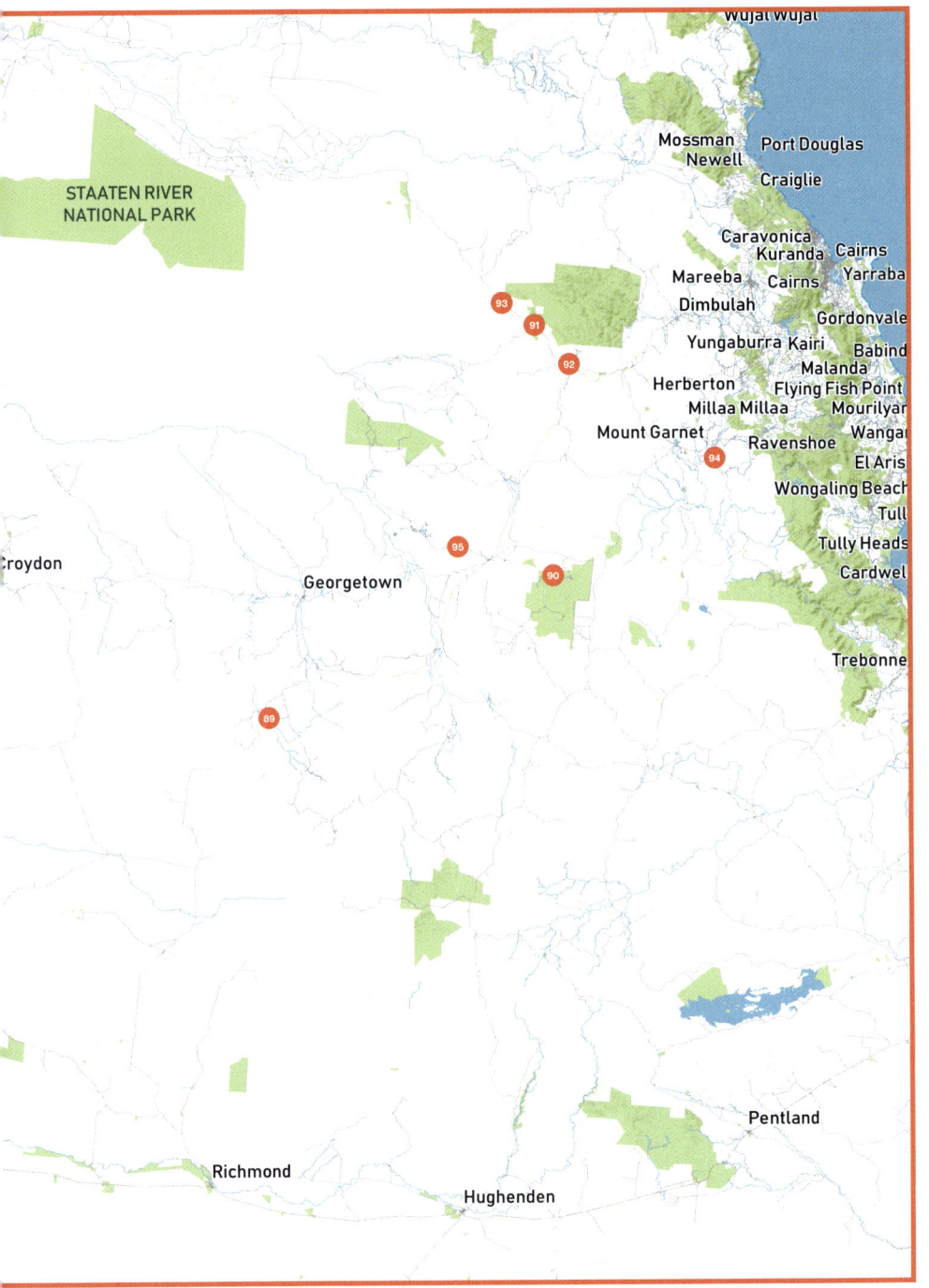

Exploring Eden Media

100 Things to See In Tropical North Queensland was first published in 2020 by Exploring Eden Media

ISBN: 978-0-6484646-2-4

Copyright

Text © Catherine Lawson and David Bristow 2020
Concept © Exploring Eden Media Pty. Ltd.
Maps @ OpenStreetMap contributors, MapTiler.

The moral rights of the author have been asserted.

All rights reserved. Except as permitted under the Australian Copyright Act 1968, no part of this book may be reproduced, stored in a retrieval system, communicated or transmitted in any form or by any means without prior written permission of the publisher or copyright holders.

All inquiries should be made to:
Exploring Eden Media Pty Ltd
250 Princes Highway, Bulli, NSW, 2516
publications@exploringedenmedia.com

A catalogue record for this book is available from the National Library of Australia

Authors: Catherine Lawson and David Bristow
Editor: Melissa Connell
Sub Editor: Brendan Batty
Design: Matthew Ware, OBJKTIVE
Cartography: Paul Buttigieg

Printed in China by 1010 Printing

Disclaimer

Some of the activities mentioned in this book are dangerous and many of the regions are wild and remote. Consider your own safety and that of your companions when undertaking travel or participating in activities referenced within, which you undertake at your own risk.

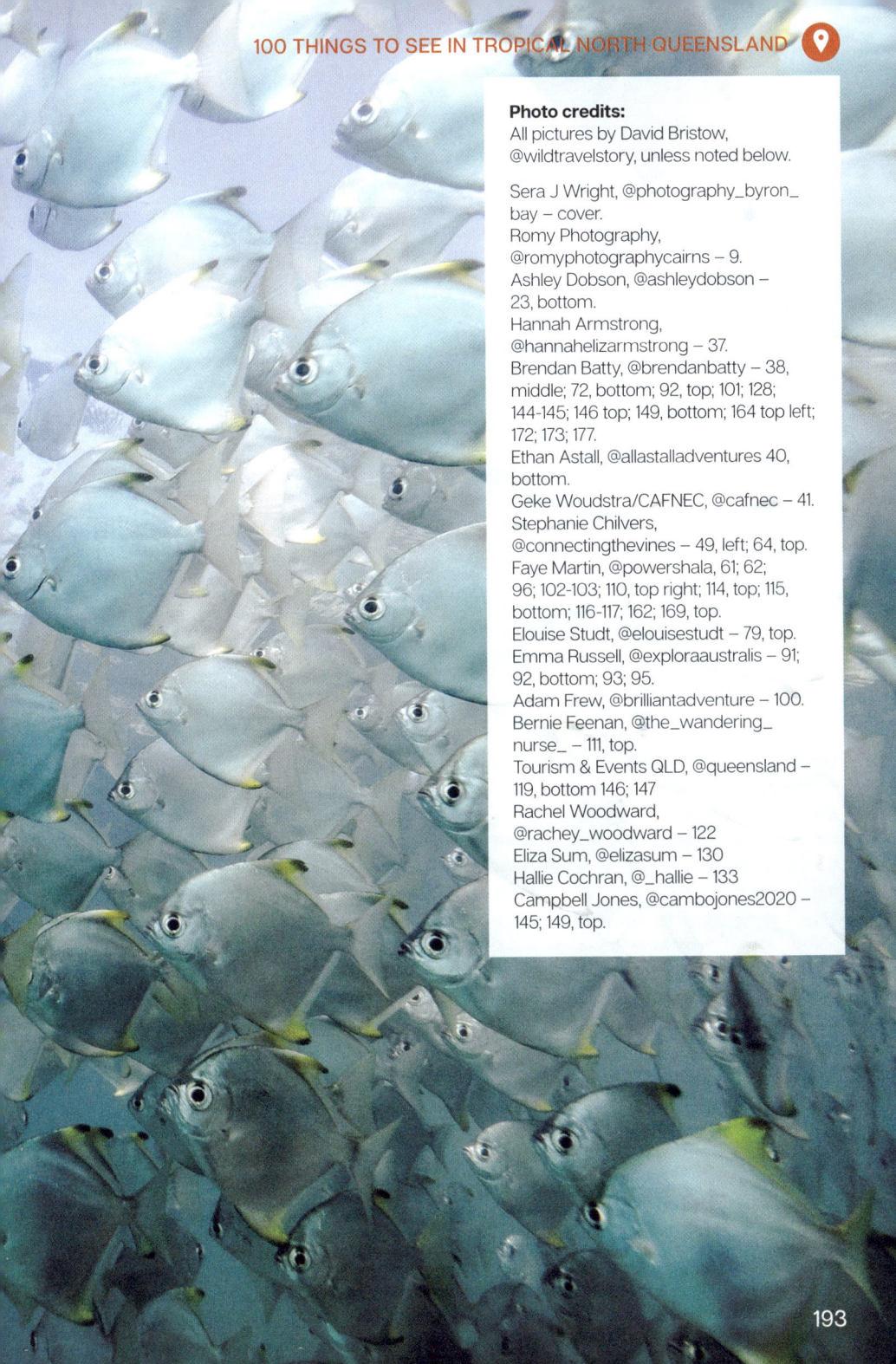

100 THINGS TO SEE IN TROPICAL NORTH QUEENSLAND

Photo credits:
All pictures by David Bristow, @wildtravelstory, unless noted below.

Sera J Wright, @photography_byron_bay – cover.
Romy Photography, @romyphotographycairns – 9.
Ashley Dobson, @ashleydobson – 23, bottom.
Hannah Armstrong, @hannahelizarmstrong – 37.
Brendan Batty, @brendanbatty – 38, bottom; 72, bottom; 92, top; 101; 128; 144-145; 146 top; 149, bottom; 164 top left; 172; 173; 177.
Ethan Astall, @allastalladventures 40, bottom.
Geke Woudstra/CAFNEC, @cafnec – 41.
Stephanie Chilvers, @connectingthevines – 49, left; 64, top.
Faye Martin, @powershala, 61; 62; 96; 102-103; 110, top right; 114, top; 115, bottom; 116-117; 162; 169, top.
Elouise Studt, @elouisestudt – 79, top.
Emma Russell, @exploraaustralis – 91; 92, bottom; 93; 95.
Adam Frew, @brilliantadventure – 100.
Bernie Feenan, @the_wandering_nurse_ – 111, top.
Tourism & Events QLD, @queensland – 119, bottom 146; 147
Rachel Woodward, @rachey_woodward – 122
Eliza Sum, @elizasum – 130
Hallie Cochran, @_hallie – 133
Campbell Jones, @cambojones2020 – 145; 149, top.

From The Authors

To everyone who has supported our family adventures without question (even when you thought we were insane), a huge Thank-You (you know who you are). All those late-night airport drop-offs, beds and meals, chats and friendship from afar mean the world to us. Finally, a big thank-you to Leonie, John, Val and Richard for trusting us to take your granddaughter far, far away and coming to see her when we do.

Catherine Lawson and David Bristow
wildtravelstory.com
@wildtravelstory

From The Publishers

Books like this aren't just the work of one or two people, and many have been very generous with their time and resourses to make this possible. We couldn't do it without the people who've been mentioned in the picture credits, for instance (follow their own adventures on Instagam), or those who offered expert advice, like the Cairns and Far North Environment Centre (cafnec.org.au - they do incredible work, check them out), or Les Hiddins, the Bush Tucker Man, who lent so much of his time to help show off his favourite part of the world.

Mostly, thank you, the readers who are exploring TNQ with this guide. Books are pointless without readers, so we hope we've inspired you to look around the next corner, or over the next hill, and take in the best bits according to the locals.

Melissa Connell and Brendan Batty
exploringedenbooks.com
@100thingstosee